Introduction

The main purpose of this study manual is to give direction and incentive to the one who wants to make a diligent study of Luke's gospel.

He who would be totally involved in the things of God must be personally acquainted with the Book of God. Hence Bible study—especially the kind that encourages searching by the student himself—is an engagement that should have top priority for all Christians. This manual is not a substitute for work; rather, it is hoped that using the manual will make your work *profitable*.

There are five main parts to each lesson of this study guide:

I. *Initial Observations.* Here you are helped to get started in your study of the passage by setting up work sheets for the analysis that follows, and making a survey of the context of the passage. Pertinent background is also studied here. Momentum is the key to progress in study, and it is important to get such a momentum early in your study.

II. *Analytical Study.* This is the key section of the lesson. Here you analyze the text of the Bible (paragraphs, sentences, words). Much help is given in the paragraphical method of study in order to give you a firm foundation for analyzing the smaller parts. The analytical chart method is also used from time to time for analysis of segments (groups of paragraphs). In this section are many questions which are intended to encourage searching and digging.

III. *Notes.* A few items are singled out in each lesson for comments related to a text already discussed.

1

IV. *Advanced Study.* Here are suggested some important subjects for further study. The subjects themselves are directly related to the passage of the lesson.

V. *Concluding Remarks.* When you come to this short section, let it be a reminder to you to review the lesson and summarize its main points.

Suggestions for Using This Manual:

1. You may want to study some lessons in two or more parts because of the length of the passage involved. (The passage of each lesson averages about two chapters.)

2. There are three basic tools for study: a good Bible text, paper and pencil.

3. Develop personal study habits that are suited to your own abilities and inclinations. The following elements are basic to effective study, whatever the method:

a. Schedule: Set aside *time*; set aside a *regular* time.

b. Desire: Guard this with all your strength.

c. Methodicalness: Avoid dabbling in a haphazard fashion; learn and apply different methods suggested.

d. Observation: See for yourself *what* the Bible says, and *how* it says it.

e. Recording: Keep your pencil busy. This is one of the main emphases of this self-study series.

f. Dependence: Look to the Spirit's enlightenment as you interpret the biblical text.

4. The following outside helps will facilitate your study:

a. One or two good modern Bible versions (for comparison with the Bible text you are using).

b. A Bible dictionary or Bible encyclopedia (especially helpful on names of people and places).

c. A harmony of the Gospels (for comparing Luke with the other three Gospels). The study book of this series, *Studies in the Life of Christ*, would also be helpful in this connection.

d. A commentary (the one-volume commentary, *The Wycliffe Bible Commentary*, is highly recommended).

Suggestions for Teachers of Bible Classes:

1. Make clear to the members of the class what you want them to do in preparation for the next meeting. Encourage them to write out answers to all questions, record paragraph titles, and jot down observations on analytical charts when these are called for.

2. Stimulate discussion during the class meeting. Encourage everyone to participate. Some can do more; some can do less; but all can do some.

3. Encourage the members to ask questions about difficult verses. Recognize problem passages in the Bible when they appear. Use these occasions to emphasize the maxim of interpretation that whatever is *essential* is *clear*.

4. If possible reproduce on a chalkboard the charts of the manual. Refer to them in the course of your class discussion. Remember the importance of the "eye gate" for teaching.

5. Devote the last part of your meeting to sharing the spiritual lessons taught by the Scripture passage. This should be the climax of the class hour.

Publisher's Note

Enlarged charts related to the lessons of this study guide are available in *Jensen Bible Study Charts* (Vol. I, General Survey; Vol. II, Old Testament; Vol. III, New Testament). The charts are especially valuable for Bible study groups.

The 8½ × 11" charts can be reproduced as Xerox copies or as transparencies for overhead projectors. Selected transparencies are included in each volume.

Background and Survey

LUKE AND JOHN ARE THE TWO GOSPEL

WRITERS WHO STATE IN THE GOSPEL TEXT

*SOMETHING OF THEIR PURPOSE IN WRITING.**

Luke, writing to his friend Theophilus, put it this way: "I thought it good to write an orderly account for you . . . so that you will know the full truth of all those matters which you have been taught."† So as Dr. Luke was inspired to write his account, the *content* he had in mind was the "full truth," and the *form* he had in mind was an "orderly account."

All survey and analytical study of the Bible text involves (1) what the Bible says (this is *content*); and (2) how it says it (this is *form*). Our analytical studies of Luke begin with Lesson 2. Survey, or a skyscraper view of the gospel, appears in the second half of this lesson. Before we make a survey, however, it will enrich our study if we first learn some of the interesting backgrounds of the book's actual writing. This study guide follows the standard order of procedure, which is

BACKGROUND	(Lesson 1)
SURVEY	(Lesson 1)
ANALYSIS	(Lessons 2 ff.)

I. BACKGROUND.

A. The Man Luke.

To know the writer of this gospel is to appreciate more fully the book he has written. From the sparse biographical data about Luke contained in the Gospels and Acts, an unusually full portrait of the man can be composed.

---

* Luke 1:1-4; John 20:30-31; 21:24-25.
† Luke 1:3-4, Good News for Modern Man.

1. BIRTH AND EARLY LIFE. Luke was born of Greek parents, a heritage that made him probably the only Gentile writer of the New Testament. He was born at about the same time as Jesus and Paul. Two possible birthplaces are Antioch of Pisidia and Philippi of Macedonia. His parents gave him the name of Lucas, a shortened form of the Roman name Lucanus.‡ His advanced education may have been received at Athens or Tarsus, where he studied for the medical profession. From the content and style of his books, we may speculate that history and literature were two of his favorite subjects.

2. CONVERSION. Luke was not a disciple of Jesus during Jesus' earthly ministry. He may have been converted under the ministry of Paul while living in Antioch, such as is referred to in Acts 11:25-26.

3. PROFESSION AND MINISTRY. Luke was a man of various talents and callings:

a. Physician. "Luke, the beloved physician" (Col. 4:14).§

b. Historian. His interest in history is shown by the many historical datelines cited in the gospel (e.g., 1:5, 26, 56; 2:1, 2, 21-22, 36-37, 42; 3:1-2).

c. Writer. His gospel is considered by many to be a literary masterpiece.

d. Evangelist and pastor. He was Paul's colaborer on the apostle's missionary journeys, remaining with him till Paul's death (read Col. 4:14; Philemon 24; II Tim. 4:11). Apparently Luke never married.

4. LUKE'S CHARACTER. Luke's writings serve as character prints. What he included and emphasized in his gospel and Acts reveals much about what kind of man he was. Luke was kind, humble, joyful, bright, pious and gentle. He had a keen sense of the might, justice and holiness of God. He was surely a man of prayer, reporting praise and intercession often in his writings. For example, read the songs recorded at 1:46-55 (Mary); 1:67-79 (Zacharias);

---

‡ Actually, the name Luke appears only three times in the New Testament, once in each of three of Paul's prison epistles: Col. 4:14; Philemon 24; II Tim. 4:11. More is known of Luke from his other book, Acts, where he is one of Paul's companions in the "we" sections.

§ Note the medical terms and descriptions of these passages: Luke 4:38-39; 8:43-44; 13:11; 16:20-21. Also it is significant that of the six miracles recorded by Luke not found in the other Gospels, five are miracles of healing: 7:11-18 (widow's son); 13:11-17 (18-year infirmity); 14:1-6 (man with dropsy); 17:11-19 (10 lepers); 22:50-51 (ear healed).

2:13-14 (angels); 2:25, 29-32 (Simeon); also, Luke's gospel refers to the prayers of Jesus more than do Matthew and Mark, and it contains three parables on prayer not found in the other Gospels. Luke was also a man of love and sympathy for the underprivileged and humble estate, such as the women, children and the poor; and for the outcasts, such as the Samaritans. He was truly a saint who identified himself with needy humankind, and thus was the very appropriate divine choice as the writer of the gospel of "The Son of Man Among Men."

5. DEATH. One tradition says Luke died as a martyr in Greece. According to the anti-Marcionite "Prologue to Luke," written around A.D. 170, "at the age of eighty-four he fell asleep in Boeotia."

B. The Book of Luke.

This gospel was inspired and written according to divine design and schedule, eventually to be listed as the forty-second book of the sixty-six-book library in the Bible. What is known of its writing? Let us look into this.

1. PLACE AND DATE OF WRITING. The place of writing is unknown; it could have been Caesarea or Rome. Luke wrote his gospel around A.D. 60, not much earlier than writing Acts (c. A.D. 61). Read Acts 1:1 for Dr. Luke's reference to his gospel as "the *former* treatise."

2. SOURCES OF INFORMATION. Luke had access to other early written records of the life and ministry of Jesus (cf. Luke 1:1-2), and he also interviewed many people who had been eyewitnesses of the events of Jesus' life (Luke 1:2). While Paul was imprisoned at Caesarea before his voyage to Rome, Luke had ample opportunity for such interviewing in the cities of Palestine. Paul himself, though not an eyewitness, must have had some influence on Luke's production of this gospel, even as Peter influenced Mark. Direct disclosure of some parts of the gospel came by the Holy Spirit; *all* of the gospel was divinely inspired, or God-breathed.

3. ADDRESSEE. Luke wrote this gospel especially for his friend Theophilus ("lover [or loved] of God"; cf. Acts 1:1; Luke 1:3). Theophilus may have been an influential Christian layman of Greece, possibly even a convert of Luke. When Luke's gospel began to circulate throughout the Roman Empire in the first century, the readers par-

ticularly attracted to it were people of Greek culture, which glorified wisdom, beauty and the ideal man. The excellent literary style of this third gospel must have afforded a special attraction to such readers.

4. PURPOSE AND THEME. As noted earlier, Luke states his purpose in 1:1-4: to write an orderly account of the full truth of Jesus' ministry. Also, in view of the fact that there are *four* Gospels instead of *one*, we may conclude that the gospel of Luke is intended to complement the other three Gospels by telling the story of Jesus from a different angle and for a different viewer. When the four Gospels are compared, differences of the following kind are seen:

COMPARISON OF FOUR GOSPELS
Chart A

	MATTHEW	MARK	LUKE	JOHN
Jesus as:	King of Israel	Servant of the Lord	Son of Man	Son of God
Reader:	Jew	Roman	Greek	World
Prominent ideas:	Law ·	Power	Grace	Glory

The theme of Luke concerns "Jesus of Nazareth, which was a prophet mighty in deed and word before God and all the people" (Luke 24:19). Luke presents Jesus as the Son of Man among men (19:10), the perfect God-Man (cf. Luke 1:35) who alone offers to all nations (24:47) the salvation of God (3:6). A key verse for Luke is 19:10: "For the Son of man is come to seek and to save that which was lost." A key phrase is "Son of man," found twenty-five times in the gospel.

We will become more aware of the purposes and theme of Luke as we proceed with our study of the actual text.

II. SURVEY.

Now that we are ready to study the actual *text* of Luke, where do we begin? The answer is, begin with the large whole, and then proceed to the small parts. The large, over-all view is known by various names: skyscraper view, bird's-eye view, overview, survey. Survey study should always precede analytical study, as stated by the rule "Image the whole, then execute the parts."

There are three main stages of survey study: (1) making the initial acquaintance; (2) scanning the prominent individual items; and (3) searching for the integrating relationships. Throughout your survey study, avoid getting bogged down in any particular details. Study of details comes later in analysis. In survey, the purpose is to see the larger things, such as general movements, turning points and highlights.

A. Stage One: Making Initial Acquaintance.

Scan the book of Luke in one sitting if possible. It is not necessary to read every word or line at this time. If your Bible has paragraph divisions, reading the first sentence of each paragraph will suffice. If your Bible has chapter or paragraph headings, note these as you scan the book.

The purpose of this initial scanning is to get the feel and atmosphere of the book and to catch its major purposes. Write down your first impressions of the book, and any key words and phrases that stand out as of this reading.

B. Stage Two: Scanning Individual Items.

1. Go through the book once again (still in cursory fashion) and assign a chapter title to each chapter. (A chapter title is a strong word or short phrase, preferably taken from the text, intended to serve as a clue to at least one

CHAPTER TITLES Chart B

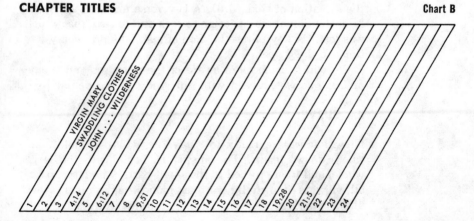

main part of the chapter. Some Bible students like to memorize the chapter titles as an aid in recalling the movement of the entire book.) Record your titles on a chart similar to Chart B. Note that 4:14; 6:12; 9:51; 19:28; and 21:5 replace 4:1; 6:1; 9:1; 19:1; and 21:1.

2. What have you noticed so far about these subjects:

the various groups Jesus spoke to and worked with_____

the constant action in the book—Jesus moving from place

to place_____

how much speaking Jesus did, compared to working_____

3. Compare the first and last chapters of the gospel. For example, note the references to praise.

C. Stage Three: Seeking Integrating Relationships.

The Gospels are not unorganized collections of the recorded words and deeds of Jesus. Each gospel is a unified story of selected parts of Jesus' life. A general chronology is followed, with some parts written mainly with a topical organization in mind.

Let us now look at the organization of Luke.

1. Observe from survey Chart D that main divisions are made at 4:14; 9:51 and 19:28. In order to understand the reasons for these divisions, we need to know the overall plan of Jesus' life; Chart C shows this. The shaded area indicates how much of Jesus' life is reported by Luke.|| Observe the locations of 4:14; 9:51; 19:28.

Read 4:14-15. Is Jesus engaged in public ministry here? Scan all that happens before 4:14, and the reason for a main division at 4:14 will become evident. Make a brief outline for these sections:

1:1—2:20 _____

|| The full biographical content of the chart is arrived at by comparing all four Gospels. No one gospel includes all the events, but Luke's gospel is regarded as the most generally representative biography. About half of its material is not found in the other Gospels.

LIFE OF CHRIST SHOWING COVERAGE BY LUKE (SHADED AREA)   Chart C

10

2:21-52 _____

3:1-20 _____

3:21-38 _____

4:1-13 _____
Now read 9:51. Note the geographical reference. It is at this point in Luke that Jesus enters the later Judean and Perean ministries (see chart) on His way to Jerusalem. Read 19:28 and justify a main division at this point in

the gospel _____

2. It is interesting to observe where in Luke most of the miracles occur, and where the parables abound. Below is a list of each group. Put in the chapter spaces of survey Chart D a check mark (√) for each miracle, a letter X (X) for each parable, and you will observe the respective concentrations.

Miracles: chap. 4: unclean demon; Simon's mother-in-law; chap. 5: fishes; leper; palsy; chap. 6: withered hand; chap. 7: centurion's servant; widow's son; chap. 8:1—9:50: sea calm; man in tombs; twelve-year issue; Jairus' daughter; 5,000 fed; unclean spirit; chap. 11: dumb devil; chap. 13: eighteen-year infirmity; chap. 14: man with dropsy; chap. 17: ten lepers healed; chap. 21: ear healed.

Parables: chap. 7: two debtors; chap. 8: sower; chap. 10: good Samaritan; chap. 11: friend at midnight; chap. 12: rich fool; chap. 13: fig tree; mustard seed; leaven; chap. 15: lost sheep; lost coin; lost son; chap. 16: unrighteous steward; chap. 17: unprofitable servants; 18:1—19:27: unjust judge; Pharisee and publican; pounds; chap. 20: wicked husbandmen; chap. 21: signs of fig tree.

Concerning the deeds (miracles) and words (parables) of Jesus, compare I Corinthians 1:22: "For the Jews require a *sign,* and the Greeks seek after *wisdom.*"

3. Study the outlines on Chart D to see how the chapters of Luke may be brought together in groups of common subject. If you choose to do more survey study, you may want to add your own outlines to this chart.

LUKE   BOOK OF THE SON OF MAN AMONG MEN

Chart D

Key verses: 19:10, 24:19
Key phrase: "Son of man"

PRAISE Chap. 1

Elizabeth—Mary

mainly peculiar to Luke

about 60% peculiar to Luke

PRAISE 24:50-53

PREPARATION	IDENTIFICATION	INSTRUCTION	SACRIFICE
1 2 3	4:14 5 6:12 7 8	9:51 10 11 12 13 14 15 16 17 18	19:28 20 21:5 22 23 24
	GALILEE	later Judean and Perean ministries TO JERUSALEM	AT JERUSALEM
	MIRACLES Abound Here	PARABLES Abound Here	the Great Sacrifice & the Grand Miracle
	"mighty in DEED →"	and WORD" (24:19)	LAST MESSAGES — MISSION ACCOMPLISHED
30 years	1½ years	6 months	8 days — 50 days

Observe from the bottom of the chart the time duration of each division of Luke. Note that the largest division (9:51 —19:27) is of only six months' duration, that this division concerns Jesus' *transient* ministry on the way to Jerusalem, and that much of these chapters is found only in Luke.

III. FURTHER DESCRIPTIONS.

Other things might be said here about the book of Luke, by way of orientation, before we launch into our analytical studies of its text. Some of these you may have observed in the course of your survey study.

A. Prominent Subjects.

The following subjects, because of their prominence in Luke, reveal something of the gospel's theme.

1. The person of Christ. Luke presents Jesus as Son of God (1:35), but especially as Son of man.

2. The work of Christ in redemption. References to grace and the glad tidings occur throughout the book. Christ is the gracious Saviour of mankind (19:10).

3. The work of the Holy Spirit. The Holy Spirit is referred to more in Luke than in Matthew and Mark combined. Read 1:15, 35, 41, 67; 2:25-26; 3:22; 4:1, 14, 18; 10:21; 24:49.

4. Christ's ministry to Gentiles. For example, read 2:32.

5. The needs of the humble estate. Women, children and outcasts appear often in Luke's story. For example, women are mentioned in all but five of the chapters.

6. Enemies of Jesus. Luke shows Jesus as One who did not spurn His many enemies but shared the truth with them.

7. Historical perspective. The *factual* basis of the gospel is underscored by the inclusion of many references to dates and secular rulers.

8. Prayers of Jesus. As mentioned earlier, prayers of Jesus are prominent throughout the book, emphasizing His humanity.

B. Special Passages.

Among other things, Luke is known for its inclusion of these three stories:

1. The "Infancy Narrative" of Jesus and John (chaps. 1—2).

2. The "Journey of Travel," also known as the "Great Insertion" (9:51—13:14).

3. The Emmaus story (chap. 24).

A list of shorter passages found only in Luke includes such accounts as:

1. Christ weeping over Jerusalem (19:41-44; cf. 13:34-35).

2. The sweat at Gethsemane (22:44).

3. Mercy to the thief on the cross (23:40-43).

* * *

Some Review Questions

1. What interesting facts have you learned in this lesson about Luke's background, profession and character? How does this knowledge help you to appreciate the gospel more fully?_____

_____

_____

_____

_____

2. Why was this gospel written?_____

_____

_____

How appropriate is it for the present times?_____

_____

3. Compare the four Gospels. _____

_____

_____

4. What is the theme of Luke's gospel?_____

_____

5. How much of the chart of Christ's life (Chart C) do you remember? What parts of His life are covered by Luke?

_____

6. Try to reproduce the survey chart (Chart D), especially its major parts. Continue studying this chart until you know it thoroughly. It will be of much help to you in the analytical studies, for context orientation.

7. What is a key phrase of Luke?_____
8. List some of the main subjects appearing in this gospel.

_____

_____

_____

9. As you conclude this study, think of some of the spiritual lessons which you have learned from your introduction to Luke.

The Births of John and Jesus

LUKE BEGINS HIS GOSPEL AS ONE MIGHT

EXPECT A HISTORIAN TO DO—DESCRIBING

BACKGROUND AND PRELIMINARY EVENTS FIRST.

He leads up to *the great event*, the coming of Jesus. In this connection it is interesting to observe that the first direct reference to Jesus is not made until verse 31 of chapter 1.* For a brief introductory exercise, make a note of the various people (whether general, like "many" of 1:1, or specific, like "Herod" of 1:5) mentioned in the first thirty verses. For those thirty verses Luke is setting the stage; and then, bursting forth in all their glory, appear the beautiful words "Thou shalt . . . bring forth a son, and shalt call his name JESUS."

I. INITIAL OBSERVATIONS.

The passage of this lesson is as weighty as it is long. If it is studied in two units, the second unit should begin at 1:57.

1. Read 1:1-4, noting especially the atmosphere of truth and authority with which this gospel opens. Consider the strength of these phrases: "many have taken in hand"; "most surely believed"; "eyewitnesses"; "ministers of the word"; "perfect understanding"; "from the very first"†; "know the certainty."

2. On Chart D the section 1:1—4:13 is called Preparation.‡ Two preparations are meant by this: the preparation of the people through the ministry of John the Baptist, and the preparation of Jesus for His public ministry. Study Chart E to see how Luke interweaves the two preparations in his account. Follow the numbers, for Luke's order.

---

* There are indirect references to the Lord in earlier verses, such as v. 17.

† This phrase translates the Greek *anothen*, which has another possible, not probable, meaning: "from above."

‡ Actually, 1:1-4, an introduction to the epistle, stands by itself.

Preparation of the People		Preparation of Jesus	
6 B.C.			
1 Announcement of John's Coming	1:5-25	2 Announcement of Jesus' Coming	1:26-56
3 Birth of John (5 B.C.)	1:57-58	4 Birth of Jesus (5 B.C.)	2:1-20
Infant John Presented in Temple	1:59-79	Infant Jesus Presented in Temple	2:21-39
Maturing Years of John	1:80	Maturing Years of Jesus	2:40-52
A.D. 26			
5 John Preaching in Wilderness	3:1-20	6 Baptism of Jesus	3:21-38
		7 Temptations of Jesus	4:1-13

3. Observe from the chart shown above the arrangement of interchange:

— announcement of John's coming   1:5-25
    — announcement of Jesus' coming   1:26-56
— birth of John   1:57 ff.
    — birth of Jesus   2:1 ff.

Keep in mind as you study 1:5—2:52 how such an arrangement emphasizes the likenesses of John and Jesus, and the differences. Which of the two birth accounts is longer?

4. Read through the passage 1:5—2:52, paragraph by paragraph, expectantly. Record your paragraph titles below:

1:5-25

    26-38

    39-56

    57-58

    59-80

2:1-7

    8-20

    21

    22-39

    40-52

What are your dominant impressions of this story?_____

What words, phrases and whole sentences stand out?_____

____

What do you consider to be the five greatest moments in
the narrative of these chapters?_____

____

____

II. ANALYTICAL STUDY.

A. The Two Announcements (1:5-56).

THE TWO ANNOUNCEMENTS

Chart F

Parents' names:	Zacharias, Elizabeth 1:5-25	Joseph, Mary 1:26-56
*commendation of parents	v. 6	vv. 28, 30
place of announcement		
angel		
the one addressed		
first reaction		
*prophecies of the sons	vv.13-17	vv. 30-33, 35
question of doubt		
angel's explanation		
wife's conclusion	v. 25	v. 38

Meeting of the two women:
  *Mary and the child are blessed (vv. 39-45)

  *Lord is magnified (vv. 46-55)

Read the two announcements and the meeting of Mary and Elizabeth with the view to making comparisons. Record your comparisons on Chart F. The subjects marked with an asterisk should be given special attention.
What does this passage teach about:

the mighty power of God_____

a walk acceptable to God_____

the preparation of hearts to hear the gospel_____

_____

the grace of God_____

the blessings of the gospel_____

the person of Christ_____

the work of Christ_____
How is Mary's "Magnificat" (vv. 46-55) a beautiful climax to this part of Luke's story?_____

_____

B. John the Baptist—from Birth to Public Ministry (1:57-80).

1. BIRTH (1:57-58). Observe how brief this story is, compared to that of Jesus (2:1-20). What bright words are prominent in these two verses?_____

_____

2. PRESENTATION IN THE TEMPLE (1:59-79). Concerning the name given Elizabeth's son, observe how tradition (v. 59b) and divine instruction (cf. v. 60 and 1:13) are at odds here. Which wins out? How does the sign of verse 64 show God's approval?_____

_____

Observe from verse 66 that already people's hearts were being prepared to listen to John's message. John's very name (from the Hebrew Yohanan, "God is gracious") would also be a continual reminder to the people that God had not forgotten the people whom He had created.

Study carefully Zacharias' "Benedictus" (vv. 68-79). Compare Malachi 4. Zacharias' words are mostly about whom?

_____

What was John's task (v. 76)?_____

What is taught in these verses about the need of salvation and the fruits of salvation?_____

_____

What is the prevailing spirit of Zacharias' words?_____

_____

Can we learn something from this for today? _____

_____

3. MATURING YEARS (1:80). What is meant by "strong in spirit"?_____

_____

How is the sovereignty of God reflected in the phrase "the day of his showing unto Israel"?_____

C. Jesus the Saviour—from Birth to Public Ministry (2:1-52).

1. BIRTH (2:1-20). The beauty of this nativity story is unsurpassed in all of literature. Do not let the familiarity of the story keep you from seeing its significant and wonderful truths.

Read 2:1-7. How is each of the following places a part of the story: Rome (Caesar Augustus was Rome's first emperor, 27 B.C.-A.D. 14), Nazareth, Bethlehem, inn, manger?

Contrast the beginning and end of this paragraph._____

_____

On the fulfillment of prophecy concerning Bethlehem, read Matthew 2:4-6 and Micah 5:2.

Read 2:8-14. What are the miracles of this paragraph?____

_____

Compare the shepherds of this paragraph with the emperor of 2:1. What is God's view of the humble estate and profession? _____

Observe the three titles of Jesus in verse 11. "Christ" means "the anointed One." What is the impact of the three titles brought together thus?___ _____

Read 14b as, "And on earth peace among men in whom he is well pleased" (ASV).

Read 2:15-20. What is the miracle of this paragraph?_____

Observe that the shepherds and the people *wondered*, while Mary *pondered*. Why did Mary have deep thought over what had transpired?_____

2. PRESENTATION IN THE TEMPLE (2:21-39). The name Jesus is the Hebrew *Jeshua,* meaning "Jehovah is salvation." Read Matthew 1:21 in this connection. Read Leviticus 12 for the Mosaic instructions followed here. Why did Jesus' parents fulfill the Mosaic law?_____

In view of 2:24 and Leviticus 12:8, what was the financial status of Joseph and Mary?_____

Study carefully the words of Simeon. What does verse 32 reveal about the gospel of Jesus Christ?_____

Note the spirit of praise and thanksgiving of Simeon and Anna.

3. MATURING YEARS (2:40-52). Luke is the sole biblical source of this thirty-year period of Jesus' life. First read verses 40 and 52 for the general descriptions; then read verses 41-51, for a selected story out of those years.

The occasion: annual Passover. This was the most important of the Jewish holidays.

Jesus' age: twelve. At twelve years a Jewish son assumed adult obligations at worship and the feasts.

Separation from parents: When the Passover services were completed, the women left the city with the first contingents of caravans. Mary probably thought her Son was with Joseph, and Joseph thought He was with Mary.

What does Jesus' interest in the temple discussions reveal about Him?_____

_____

What was Jesus' persuasion concerning His relation to the heavenly Father?_____

_____

To what extent did He submit to parental authority (v. 51)?_____

_____

What is suggested by the phrase "in favor with God and man" (v. 52)?_____

_____

How does verse 40 describe the healthy maturing of a well-rounded person?_____

_____

Why do you think the Holy Spirit of God inspired Luke to include this story in his gospel?_____

_____

III. NOTES.

1. "Espoused to a man" (1:27). Such betrothal was more binding than present-day engagements. Of this *The Wycliffe Bible Commentary* says,

> The Jewish law held espousal or engagement to be as binding as marriage. An engagement was completed after negotiations had been carried on by the groom's representative and the dowry money had been paid to the girl's father. After the betrothal, the groom could claim the bride at any time. The legal aspect of marriage was included in the betrothal.§

§ Charles F. Pfeiffer and Everett F. Harrison (eds.), *The Wycliffe Bible Commentary* (Chicago: Moody, 1962), pp. 1030-31.

2. "The mother of my Lord" (1:43). Mary, the mother of Jesus, was honored by Elizabeth and the angel Gabriel, but she was not worshiped by them, nor by any others in the Christmas story, nor by Jesus. In fact, she refused to call attention to herself, meditating privately over the honor of being Jesus' mother, and only magnifying Jesus as her Lord and Saviour (1:46-55).

3. The date of Christmas. The year of Jesus' birth was 6 or 5 B.C.|| The exact day of the year is unknown. December 25 is merely a legendary date, traced back to the fourth century.

IV. ADVANCED STUDY.

1. Worship of God is a prominent subject of these first two chapters of Luke. Extend your study of this subject to other passages in the Bible, using such helps as a concordance, commentary and encyclopedia. Consider such areas as the true object of worship; way of access to God; heart attitudes; forms of public worship; fruits of worship; idolatry. Some Bible passages to be read are: Isaiah 2:8; I Kings 11:33; Psalm 95:6; I Chronicles 29:20; Isaiah 44:17; Matthew 4:8-10; Exodus 20:5; Hebrews 8:5; 10:20; I Timothy 2:5; I Peter 2:9; Revelation 4; Psalm 96:9; John 4:20-26; Psalm 100:4-5; Hebrews 10:24-25; Philippians 2:9-11; Revelation 5:5-14; 7:9-12; Psalm 27:4.

2. The virgin birth and deity of Christ are other important truths taught by Luke. Before referring to other books of the Bible, observe carefully all that Luke records to substantiate these truths.

V. CONCLUDING REMARKS.

One cannot leave these chapters of Luke without a sense of renewed gratitude for God's gift of His Son and for the blessing of knowing Him as personal Saviour. Simeon's touching words were one way of expressing such gratitude:

> Lord, now lettest thou thy servant depart
> In peace, according to thy word:
> For mine eyes have seen thy salvation (2:29-30).

|| Consult a Bible encyclopedia for discussion of the error giving rise to the present calendar of years.

The Preaching of John, and Baptism and Temptations of Jesus

LUKE WRITES WITH THE PRECISION OF A

HISTORIAN, CREATIVITY OF A COMPOSER,

AND HUMAN COMPASSION OF A PHYSICIAN.

This is particularly true as he describes for us the story of the births of John the Baptist and Jesus (chaps. 1—2). He also briefly mentions their growing and maturing through the stages of infancy to manhood. Now Luke continues his narrative in detail at the point where John the Baptist, about age thirty, begins his public ministry, followed shortly by Jesus.

In the first two chapters of Luke, we have been reading how John came on the scene first, followed by Jesus. People rejoiced when John was born, as well as when Jesus was born. But there was everything about the narrative that spotlighted *Jesus* as the main Person, the source of all blessing. Now again, in the passage of this lesson, John comes on the scene first, followed by Jesus. Here John can speak for himself, and what he has to say focuses all attention on the One whom he precedes, as he speaks thus of Christ: "One mightier than I cometh, the latchet of whose shoes I am not worthy to unloose" (3:16).

I.   INITIAL OBSERVATIONS.

1.   First, mark off paragraph divisions in your Bible. See Chart G for the locations of these divisions.
2.   With pencil in hand, read through the passage, underlining key words and phrases as they impress you. Train your eyes to detect *strong phrases of spiritual significance* in the midst of otherwise factual data. Consider, for example, the phrase "the word of God came unto John" (3:2).

3. Record the key words and phrases on an analytical chart similar to Chart G.# Such a chart will serve as a work sheet for your observations and interpretations. As an "eye gate" device, the chart will help you see emphases and relations in the biblical text, and it will also serve as a permanent record of your growing list of observations.

4. What paragraphs are mainly about John?_____

_____

What paragraphs are mainly about Jesus?_____

_____

Where is John at the end of the John section?_____

_____

Where is Jesus at the end of the Jesus section?_____

_____

5. How is 3:21 a transitional verse, connecting what follows with what goes before?_____

_____

II. ANALYTICAL STUDY.

1. Observe the main topical study on Chart G. The key center is "One Mightier than I Cometh." The master title is "The Mighty Jesus." Read the paragraph points, beginning with No. 1, Announced by John, observing what phrase in the biblical text is the basis for the paragraph point. Try making a different topical study for this passage on the basis of a different key center.

2. The Witness of Salvation. Read 3:1-6. Observe the many references to political and religious rulers in the first two verses. How does such a context accentuate the phrase "the word of God came unto John" (3:2)?_____

_____

In the same manner, compare "wilderness" (v. 2) with the geographical references of these verses.

A detailed discussion of the analytical chart method is given in Irving L. Jensen, *Independent Bible Study* (Chicago: Moody, 1963).

THE MIGHTY JESUS

3:1—4:13

(1)	ANNOUNCED BY JOHN	1 *word of God* *came unto John*	The Witness of Salvation —word —person
(2)	TESTER OF FRUITS	7	The Test of Salvation
(3)	BRINGER OF SALVATION	15 *One mightier than I cometh*	The Saviour of Salvation John in Prison JOHN ↑
(4)	SON OF GOD	21	Jesus' Baptism
(5)	SON OF MAN	23 ... 38	Jesus' Genealogy
(6)	VICTOR OVER SATAN	4:1 ... 13	Jesus' Temptations Jesus in Wilderness JESUS ↑

26

Study the mission and message of John (vv. 3-6). What was his mission (vv. 4-5)?_____

_____

What does it mean to smooth the rough ways?_____

_____

In what way is a *prepared* heart open to the gospel?_____

_____

What was John's message (v. 3)?_____

_____

Was this a message of salvation or of preparation?_____

_____

What was the ultimate purpose of John's ministry (v. 6)?

_____

_____

3. The Test of Salvation. Read 3:7-14. John anticipates the people's claim on which they based their salvation. What was it (v. 8)?_____

_____

Then he identified the real test. What was it (vv. 9-14)? (Cf. Matt. 7:20.)_____
Was John preaching works as a way of salvation? Explain.

_____

_____

4. The Saviour of Salvation. Read 3:15-20. What is revealed about Christ in verses 15-17?_____

_____

Read Acts 2 for the fulfillment of the prophecy on the Spirit's baptism. In interpreting the meaning of baptism of fire, observe the work of fire in verse 17. Is such fire still future?_____

5. Jesus' Baptism. Read 3:21-22. What was the purpose of Jesus' baptism?_____

_____

What happened while He was praying?_____

_____

What blessed spiritual truth is illustrated by this?_____

_____

What spiritual truths are suggested by the words "heaven," "dove" and "voice"?_____

_____

Examine carefully the words of the Father to the Son. What words are about Jesus' *person*?_____

_____

What words are about His *work*?_____

_____

How do you account for the fact that such vital messages by God, recorded in the Bible, are so brief?_____

_____

6. Jesus' Genealogy. Read 3:23-38. Why does Luke record this paragraph?_____

_____

Observe that Luke traces Jesus' line back to Adam (v. 38).

How does this emphasize the humanity of Christ?_____

_____

It may be pointed out here that Matthew's list, found in Matthew 1:1-17, gives the legal line of Jesus' royal descent, while Luke gives His human line on Mary's side.**
7. Jesus' Temptations. Read 4:1-13. Focus your study of this paragraph on the following subjects:

** Heli (Luke 3:23) was apparently the father of Mary. See Irving L. Jensen, *Studies in the Life of Christ* (Chicago: Moody, 1969), Lesson 1, for a discussion of this subject.

a.   Areas of the temptations. Are they the same for people living today? Compare I John 2:16._____

_____

b.   Jesus' answers. Observe the basic principles for living contained in these answers. Note Jesus' use of Scripture. Read Ephesians 6:17.

c.   Satan's challenges of Jesus' deity. Why did Satan want Jesus to declare an independence of God?_____

_____

Make a study of references to Jesus' humanity and deity in the last three paragraphs of this segment. Record your findings on Chart H.

JESUS' HUMANITY AND DEITY

Chart H

Passage	Humanity	Deity
3:21-22		
3:23-38		
4:1-13		

d.   Jesus, "full of the Holy Ghost . . . was led [literally, 'driven'] by the Spirit into the wilderness." What is meant by this, and what are the spiritual lessons taught?_____

_____

e.   Jesus was "tempted of the devil." Some people say that Jesus' temptations were not real because He did not yield to any. What do you think?_____

_____

Who knows the full fury of Satan's onslaughts: the one who emerges the victor, or the one who goes down in defeat? Why? _____

f. "The devil departed . . . for a season." What does this suggest? _____

_____

When in the experience of Jesus did Satan become a conquered foe?_____

_____

8. What are some of the most pertinent practical lessons you have learned in your study of these chapters?_____

_____

_____

_____

_____

III. NOTES.

1. "The word of God came unto John" (3:2). This is a typical Bible phrase used for the call of a prophet. Compare Hosea 1:1; Joel 1:1; Jonah 1:1; Micah 1:1.
2. "Make his paths straight" (3:4b). In Bible times, when a high official was scheduled to ride through an area on his chariot, servants went ahead to clear the road of obstacles, and level it off if necessary. This is a very appropriate picture of John's task to "prepare . . . the way of the Lord" (3:4).
3. "Jesus . . . was led . . . into the wilderness" (4:1). The traditional site of this wilderness is the barren wasteland bordering the northwest end of the Dead Sea.

IV. ADVANCED STUDY.

1. The passage of this lesson is about two persons: John the Baptist and Jesus. On the basis of this passage alone, compare these two, looking for contrasts as well as like-

nesses._____

2. Compare the wilderness temptations of Jesus with the temptations of Adam and Eve (Gen. 3:1-7). What areas of

life were involved in the temptations?_____

_____

What is the comforting practical truth of Jesus' victory?

(Read Heb. 2:17-18; 4:14-16.)_____

_____

V. CONCLUDING REMARKS.

Throughout His earthly ministry Jesus was very aware of His relation to His Father (cf. 3:22) and to the Holy Spirit. Concerning the latter, Luke refers often to the Spirit in connection with Jesus' ministry. In this passage we saw the Spirit upon Jesus (3:22), in Him (4:1a), before Him (4:1b), and from Him (3:16). As we move into the next lesson, the very first line of Luke's continuing narrative is this: "And Jesus returned *in the power of the Spirit* into Galilee" (4:14a).

Jesus' Message Identified, Demonstrated and Opposed

WE HAVE STUDIED THE PREPARATIONS FOR

JESUS' PUBLIC MINISTRY, SEEING HOW

GOD USED JOHN THE BAPTIST IN THIS.

We also read of the experiences of Jesus which prepared Him for His approaching public ministry.

Now at 4:14 the first of Luke's reporting of Jesus' *extensive* public ministry begins. Actually, Luke skips over the events of Jesus' first-year Judean ministry, and commences at the early Galilean period. This is shown on Chart I (shaded area indicates Luke's coverage):*

CHRIST'S PUBLIC MINISTRY   Chart I

On the survey Chart D we called the section 4:14—9:50 "Identification," because during this time Jesus was trying to establish His true identity for the sake of the multitudes.

Chart J, an excerpt from survey Chart D, indicates that miracles of Jesus abound in the division 4:14—9:50.

* Of the four Gospels, only John records the early ministry in Judea (John 2:13—4:3). (Refer back to Chart C for a review of the chronology.)

32

1:1	4:14	9:51	19:28	24:53
PREPARATION	IDENTIFICATION	INSTRUCTION	SACRIFICE	
	Miracles Abound Here	Parables Abound Here		

Miracles begin to appear in the passage of this lesson, but only after Jesus has clearly identified His *person* and His *message*. The miracles are the proofs that Jesus' *message* was from above. As we study 4:14—6:11, we will pay special attention to that message in Jesus' teaching and preaching.

I. INITIAL OBSERVATIONS.

1. Chart K shows the paragraph divisions of this passage. As you read the passage paragraph by paragraph, make notations on the chart, identifying subjects, places, people and similar items.

Deeds (miracles) and words (teaching, preaching, calling) appear alternately throughout the passage. But general concentrations are identifiable, which is the basis for the outline shown at the bottom of the chart: Message Identified—Message Demonstrated—Message Opposed. Keep these outlines in mind as you analyze the passage in detail.

2. Contrast the opening verse (4:14) with the closing verse (6:11).

3. Go through the entire passage noting all the references, direct or indirect, to Jesus' *words*. Complete a progressive outline for this subject, using the following verses and any others you may choose:

4:22   gracious words

4:32

4:36

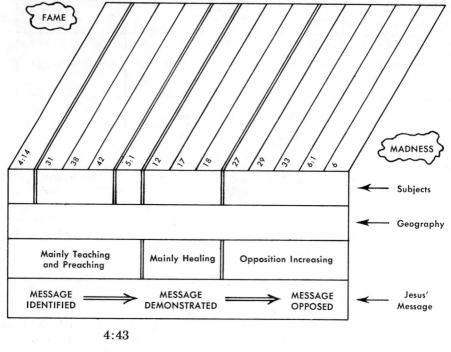

4:43

5:1

5:20

5:36

II. ANALYTICAL STUDY.

In all analytical study, work mostly with one basic Bible
version. But it is recommended that you refer continually
to at least one good modern version for the light it throws
on words and phrases in the text.
1.   Read 4:14-30. If you are studying in a group, discuss
the words "power," "fame" and "glorified" (vv. 14-15).
Study the Isaiah passage which Jesus read. Read Isaiah
61:1-2 to see where Jesus ended His reading of the prophet.
Observe the repetition of the phrase "to preach." Compare
4:43-44. Explain "gracious words" (v. 22). For background

to verse 23*b*, read John 4:46-54. Do you think Jesus was grieved not to be accepted by his own countrymen (v. 24)? How do you account for this strange human law of disaffection? _____

_____

What was Jesus saying in verses 25-27 which angered the people? _____

_____

(Observe these key pairs of the two illustrations: Israel, Sidon; and Israel, Syria.) Contrast verses 29 and 30._____

_____

Observe the fantastic miracle of verse 30, a miracle almost hidden in the gospel story.
2. Read 4:31-44. The people were impressed with Jesus' message. Was it *what* He said, or *how* He said it, or both? What was the common testimony of the evil spirits in 4:34 and 4:41?_____

_____

What was the source of their knowledge?_____

_____

Why did Jesus suppress such true testimony (v. 41)?___

_____

What may have been the main reason for the people's plea of verse 42?_____

_____

In view of this, why are His words "I must *preach*" (v. 43) so significant?_____

_____

3. Read 5:1-11. Observe among other things the *sequence* of events:

People		Jesus	
1 SEEKING (v. 1)			
		2 TEACHING (vv. 2-3)	
		3 MIRACLE-WORKING (vv. 4-7)	
4 CONFESSING (vv. 8-10a)			
		5 CALLING (v. 10b)	
6 FOLLOWING (v. 11)			

Derive some valuable practical lessons from your observations. Note, for instance, that the story moves from *seeking* to *following*. What happened in between?_____

_____

4.   Read 5:12-26. Most of these verses are about Christ at work. What verse tells of Christ at prayer?_____

What is the relation between work and prayer in the church today?_____

What may be learned from these passages:
"If thou *wilt*, thou canst" (v. 12)_____

"He saw *their* faith" (v. 20)_____

"Thy sins are forgiven thee" (v. 20)_____

What was the purpose of Jesus' directions in verse 14? (Cf. Lev. 14:1-32.)_____

Observe the opposition groups watching (v. 17) and objecting among themselves (v. 21). What divine power of Jesus is demonstrated in verse 22?_____

_____

Observe how Jesus identifies Himself in verse 24, and who was glorified in verses 25 and 26.

5. Read 5:27—6:11. This passage of Luke shows opposition to Jesus growing in intensity to the point where the enemy faction conferred among themselves how they might destroy Him. How quickly and tragically popularity can give way to opposition! It is interesting to read that one challenge arose on the occasion of a festive gathering hosted by the new convert and disciple, Levi.

Make a comparative study of the four cases of opposition (5:30-32; 5:33-39; 6:1-5; 6:6-11). For each case, observe the following:

a. Who the objectors were.

b. To whom they raised the objection.

c. About whom the objection was.

d. The objection itself.

e. Jesus' answer. In your own words, state the timeless, universal principle of Jesus' answer, applicable to today.

6. As you think back over the entire passage of this lesson, what are the dramatic moments and the key utterances of its narrative? Write down at least five vital spiritual lessons you have learned in your study of this passage.

_____

_____

_____

_____

_____

_____

Think of ways you could share these lessons with others. Then do something about it.

III. NOTES.

1. "He taught in their synagogues" (4:15). The synagogues were the meeting places for the Jewish worship

services. Synagogues originated during the time of the Babylonian captivity, after the temple had been destroyed.
2. "Levi" (5:27). Levi is another name for Matthew (Matt. 9:9), a wealthy tax agent.
3. "Children of the bridechamber" (5:34). These were the friends of the bridegroom.

IV. ADVANCED STUDY.

1. To appreciate more fully the many situations recorded by Luke involving the scribes and Pharisees, consult a Bible dictionary for a description of these groups—their customs, rites, and views on authority and salvation. Also, inquire into the occupation of publicans. Account for the common phrase "publicans and sinners" (e.g., 5:30).
2. We learn from 5:12—6:11 what Jesus' views were on various aspects of the Mosaic law. Matthew records Jesus as saying, "I am not come to destroy [the law], but to fulfil" (Matt. 5:17). Study this Luke passage in light of these words of Jesus.

V. CONCLUDING REMARKS.

The enemies of Christ, hoping to immobilize Him and His army, incessantly plotted "what they might do *to* Jesus" (6:11). Jesus, on the other hand, communed with His Father what He might do *for* His enemies (cf. 6:12). The striking quality of the gospel is its *grace*, and he who finds grace in its fullest measure has found Christ.

Middle Galilean Ministry Begins

THE TEMPO OF ANGER AND FURY IN THE

HEARTS OF THE RELIGIONISTS AGAINST

JESUS WAS NOW RAPIDLY INCREASING.

But the Man of Galilee, grieved though not distracted, proceeded with His public ministry "on schedule." At 4:30 Luke casually reports that Jesus "went his way" when the people tried to murder Him. At 6:12, the opening verse of our present lesson, Luke records, in contraposition to the preceding verse about a murder plot (6:11), that Jesus went out to a mountain to pray to God. What composure, and what triumphant spirit!

As the passage of this lesson opens, Jesus begins what is called the Middle Galilean period, almost midway in His three-year public ministry (see Chart C). Jesus' work at this time is especially full and varied, accomplished at a vigorous pace. All the time, the Son of Man is interested in people, an emphasis which Luke preserves in these chapters of his gospel.

I. INITIAL OBSERVATIONS.

(Note: this passage may be studied in two units, if desired: 6:12-49; 7:1-50).

1.   Following methods of study established in this study guide, make one or two survey readings of this passage. Record paragraph titles on Chart L, and look for groupings of paragraphs according to similar content. Compare your outline with the one shown on Chart L.

2.   Where do healings occur in the passage? Mark this on the chart.

Choosing Directors for a Special Work		Instructing Disciples How to Live in This World					Helping Distressed Ones in Their Need		Honoring Devotees		
6:12	6:17	20	27	39	43	46	7:1	11	7:18	24	36
12		many					a few		2		

3. Note how many people are directly involved with Jesus in the four sections shown on the chart.

4. Compare briefly the main persons and situations involved in the last four paragraphs:

Centurion _____

Widow _____

John the Baptist _____

Woman _____

II. ANALYTICAL STUDY.

1. Read 6:12-16. What are the prominent truths of this

paragraph? _____

_____

_____

Observe the reference to *two* groups in verse 13. Try answering these three "why" questions (the text itself does not furnish explicit answers):

Why did Jesus pray *all night* long?_____

_____

Why did Jesus need a select, small group of apostles?___

Why did Jesus choose Judas Iscariot, whom He knew would betray Him?_____

2. Read 6:17-49. The sermon beginning at verse 20 is sometimes called the "Sermon on the Plain" (from "plain" of v. 17), distinguishing it from the Sermon on the Mount of Matthew 5—7 (from "mountain," Matt. 5:1). Actually, the plain (or "level place," which is an accurate translation of the Greek) could have been on the side of the mountain, with Matthew and Luke recording the same occasion.†

What evidence is there that the twelve apostles were primary listeners to this sermon (cf. v. 17)?_____

Were the multitudes also part of the audience?_____

Why would the training of the twelve, begun here, loom so prominently in Jesus' ministry?_____

Observe the reference to healing in 6:17-19. What is the significance of such a ministry being accomplished in these contexts:

(1) after prayer_____

(2) after calling the twelve_____

(3) just before Jesus' sermon?_____

Study carefully the sermon itself. It is a mine of priceless gems. The more you look, the more you will discover. Set up on a piece of paper a work sheet similar to Chart

† For an able defense of this latter view, see A. T. Robertson, *A Harmony of the Gospels* (Nashville: Broadman, 1922), pp. 273-76.

M, and record your observations for each of the three sections:

OBSERVATIONS ON JESUS' SERMON

6:20-26	*Beatitudes and Woes*
6:27-38	*Commands*
6:39-49	*Parables and Illustrations*

Observe Jesus' emphasis on love; works; the future. Make a study of the promises and warnings of this sermon. How should one apply this sermon to today? Does it show unbelievers how to be saved, or instruct believers how to live the Christian life?

3. Read 7:1-17. Compare these two instances of Jesus' miracle-working, as to the following:
   a. the ones distressed, and extent of distress
   b. the place of faith
   c. a distinguishing mark of Jesus' power (cf. vv. 7-8 and vv. 14-15)
   d. a recorded effect on the people

Concerning the centurion, compare the commendation "he was worthy" (v. 4) with his own attitude "I am not worthy" (v. 6). What are your thoughts about mercy and merit? _____

_____

4. Read 7:18-50. What are the two main stories of this passage? _____

_____

The stories themselves seem very different from each other, but when a comparative study is made, some interesting

AN INQUIRY
answered by

18 Art thou he that should come?   (John)

DEMONSTRATION →   . . . he cured many

24

JOHN THE BAPTIST

Jesus commends John

—rebukes the people

A CHALLENGE
answered by

36 If he were a prophet,
    he would have known   (Simon)

WOMAN

Jesus rebukes Simon

—commends the woman

DEMONSTRATION →   Thy sins are forgiven

50

comparisons show up. Use Chart N for recording your observations.

Observe how Jesus answered John's inquiry (v. 19) by a demonstration (vv. 21-22); and Simon's challenge (v. 39) by a demonstration (vv. 47-48). Study also Jesus' rebukes of the people and of Simon, and His commendations of John the Baptist and of the woman.

The inquiry of John (v. 19) appears unexpectedly in the text, because the last we read of John he was preaching Jesus as Messiah with vigor and conviction. (See 3:15-18, noting especially that at that time it was the *people* who were wondering "whether he [Jesus] were the Christ, or not.") In the meantime, however, John was imprisoned by Herod (3:20). How may this explain the question that had arisen in John's mind at 7:19? (Read 7:23 thus: "How happy is he who has no doubts about me!" Good News for

Modern Man.) _____

_____

From verses 24-28, what was Jesus' estimate of John?_____

_____

Study 7:29-35 carefully to determine Jesus' indictment against the unbelieving generation. Refer to a modern version for the meaning of "justified God" (v. 29) and of verse 35.

In studying 7:36-50, look for practical teachings about genuine love, gratitude, devotion, contrition and forgiveness. "Thy faith hath saved thee" (7:50) is a simple but

profound statement. What does it mean to be saved?_____

_____

Who saves? _____
In view of this, how is faith a reasonable *way* of salvation?

_____

_____

5. As you come to the end of your analytical study, think of the profitable spiritual lessons taught by this passage of Scripture. Record some of these below. (Aim at similar applications for other lessons as well.)

examples to follow

sins to avoid

commands to obey

promises to claim

prayers to echo

III. NOTES.

1. Luke's list of twelve apostles (6:14-16) agrees essentially with the lists of Matthew (10:2-4), Mark (3:16-19) and Acts (1:13).† Judas (brother of James) of Luke's lists is the same as Thaddaeus of the other lists.

2. Luke's reporting of Jesus' sermon (6:20-49) is more condensed than Matthew's (Matt. 5—7). Among the differences are these: (1) Luke records four beatitudes with four woes; Matthew, nine beatitudes. (2) Luke omits a discussion of the application of the law (e.g., Matt. 5:13-48), and some teachings on prayer (e.g., Matt. 6:1-18).

IV. ADVANCED STUDY.

1. You may want to make a detailed comparative study of Jesus' Sermon on the Mount, as recorded by Luke and Matthew. Use a harmony of the Gospels to facilitate your study.

2. Study the passage of this lesson to see how the words spoken and the events transpiring contributed to the training of the twelve for their future ministry of carrying on Christ's work after He ascended to heaven.

3. Make a topical study of love, beginning with these passages of this lesson: 6:27-38; 7:11-17; and 7:36-50. What

is love?_____

---

† See *ibid.*, pp. 271-73, for a discussion of the four lists.

What are the qualities of God's love, and how are these an example to us as to how we should love?_____

_____

Who are objects of genuine love?_____

_____

_____

What are the fruits of love?_____

_____

_____

In your study, read the following passages: I Corinthians 13; I John 4:7-21; Matthew 22:35-40; John 3:16.

V. CONCLUDING REMARKS.

Faith and *love*—these were two of the basic qualities sought by Jesus in the hearts of men and women.

> Love your enemies.
> Thy faith hath saved thee.

If we are Christ's followers—Christians—we would do well to examine our hearts to see how much there is of that which gladdens *His* heart.

The Last Months of Jesus' Galilean Ministry

THE CLOSING WEEKS OF JESUS' GALILEAN

MINISTRY* MARKED A TURNING POINT IN

HIS REDEMPTIVE PROGRAM FOR THE MASSES.

In Luke's gospel, the verse 9:51 begins the new phase, with Jesus setting His face to go to Jerusalem to be crucified. This is illustrated in Chart O.

JESUS PRESENTING AND OFFERING HIMSELF   Chart O

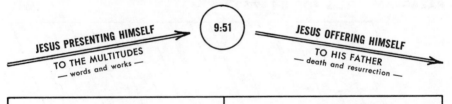

2½ years	½ year

It will be seen from the chart that most of Jesus' public ministry has been covered before Luke has reached even the midpoint of his gospel. This illustrates the feature of selectivity in the gospel's content, whereby certain subjects, such as the passion, are given special emphasis by extensive coverage.

The passage of this lesson is the last of the Galilee section of Luke (see Chart D). In our study of its paragraphs we will observe Jesus instructing, performing miracles, and training the twelve apostles, with the view to the fast-approaching day of sacrifice on Calvary. In a very real sense Jesus had reached a peak in His public ministry

* See Chart C showing the early, middle and later Galilean periods.

during these latter months of the Galilean period. When He miraculously fed the five thousand (9:10-17), the people wanted to take Him by force and make Him king (John 6:14-15). Tragically, they had misinterpreted His message, for He did not come to be the king of bread but the King of righteousness. His kingdom was not of this world. In fact, He first had to be the slain Lamb before He could be the adored King.

I. INITIAL OBSERVATIONS.

1. Before reading 8:1—9:50, study Chart C to be sure you know what parts of Jesus' ministry are reported by this passage. Observe, for example, that a fair portion of the specialized ministry, which would fall chronologically between 9:17 and 9:18, is not reported by Luke.

2. Proceed with your reading, paragraph by paragraph, to become acquainted with the narrative as Luke has put it together. Secure paragraph titles, and record them on Chart P:

PARAGRAPH TITLES FOR 8:1—9:50   Chart P

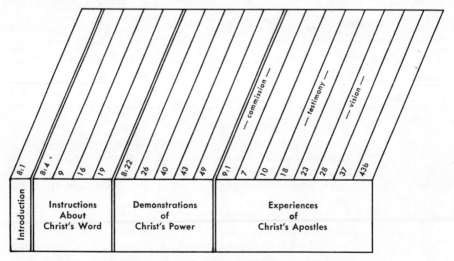

3. How is 8:1-3 introductory to this section?_____

_____

What paragraphs record miracles?_____

48

What paragraphs record teaching by Jesus? Mark these on the chart. Observe the concentrations of each.

4. From your own observations, identify groupings of paragraphs according to similar content. Study also the outline shown above.

5. Observe the three experiences of Christ's apostles, as indicated by the chart (commission, testimony, vision). In what ways were these new and vital experiences for the apostles, preparing them for the months and years to come?

_____

_____

_____

II. ANALYTICAL STUDY.

1. Read 8:1-3. What was the geographical coverage of this evangelistic tour?_____

_____

Does the fact that Luke records that "the twelve were with him" at this time suggest that they did not always travel with Him? Note Luke's reference to women. Verse 3b is one of the few verses reporting sources of Jesus' material support during His ministry.

2. Read 8:4-21. Note that the four paragraphs are about two main subjects:

THE SOWN WORD: 8:4-8; 8:9-15

THE HEARING: 8:16-18; 8:19-21

Organize your study around these two subjects.

THE SOWN WORD (8:4-15). For the parable of the sower (really, this is a parable about the *soils*), record the following:

The Parable	Jesus' Interpretation
Seed	
Wayside	
Rock	
Thorns	
Good ground	

Can you think of situations today where the hearers of the gospel are like the three unfruitful places: wayside, rock, thorns?_____

_____

_____

What are some important lessons on Christian witness to the lost which are taught by this parable?_____

_____

_____

What kind of hearing is fruitful?_____

_____

What is a parable?_____

According to verse 10, why did Jesus teach in parables? In answering this, consider Matthew 13:10-17; 13:34-35.

_____

The multitudes were not understanding the mysteries of this "new" message of the gospel. They were seeing, but they did not see. They were hearing, but they did not understand. So Jesus taught in parables not to hide truth, but to reveal it. "He gave them parabolic pictures, so that they might enquire. The purpose of the story, the picture, was to lure them to think, in order that they might find their way into the higher mystery."† (Read the three parables of Luke 15 in light of this parabolic method of Jesus.)

THE HEARING (8:16-21). Read the two paragraphs again, noting the emphasis on *hearing*. Concerning the first paragraph, observe that verse 16 gives the illustration, verse 17 gives the interpretation, and verse 18 gives the application ("therefore"). What is the impact of the phrase "how

† G. Campbell Morgan, *The Parables and Metaphors of Our Lord* (Westwood, N. J.: Revell, 1943), p. 16.

ye hear"? For your answer, use verses 21 and 15._____

_____

Have you observed that abilities and talents from God increase in proportion to their use? What do verses 16-18 reveal about parables, their purposes, and their demands?

_____

What do you think was the spirit in which Jesus spoke the words of verse 21?_____

In addition to the lesson about *hearing*, what important truth about His own mission was He teaching here?_____

Compare Mark 3:20-35 as you study this paragraph.
3. Read 8:22-56. The four miracles recorded here are demonstrations of Christ's power. Over what did He exercise His power in each instance? What did such demonstrations have to do with His teaching ministry?_____

For each of the four miracles, record the items listed on Chart Q:

THE FOUR MIRACLES OF 8:22-56   Chart Q

Subject	Storm vv. 22-25	Demoniac vv. 26-39	Issue of Blood vv. 43-48	Jairus' Daughter vv. 40-42; 49-56
Realm of miracle	nature			
Occasion				
Persons involved				
Appeal made				
Faith demonstrated				
Manner and extent of miracle				
Effect				
Main instruction of the miracle				

What are some of the major spiritual lessons taught by this passage? _____

_____

_____

4. Read 9:1-17. As you read, think especially of the twelve apostles, whom Jesus was training for the ministry of the gospel. Three main experiences of the apostles are described in 9:1-50: commission (9:1-6); testimony (9:18-27); and vision (to three apostles, 9:28-36).

Luke doesn't mention the apostles in the second paragraph (vv. 7-9), though it is obvious that their healing ministry (v. 6) was associated in the people's minds with the healings by Jesus. What twofold ministry did the apostles engage in, according to 9:1-6?_____

_____

What service were they told to render in 9:12-17?_____

_____

Make comparisons of the three ministries: preaching, healing, feeding. Which one is directly related to the eternal spirit of a man?_____

How would the other two ministries be related to the first ministry? _____

_____

Account for the instructions of 9:3-5._____

_____

Why did Luke include 9:7-9 in his story?_____

_____

Observe the qualities of practical concern, orderliness and simplicity in Jesus, in the story of the miraculous feeding. What was the procedure of distribution, according to verse

16*b*? _____

_____

What did Jesus have in mind in favor of the apostles, by

this procedure?_____

_____

What spiritual truth is illustrated by the *surplus* twelve

baskets (9:17)?_____

_____

_____

Reflect on the truths residing in these phrases, in their
context:

        "He . . . gave them power"   (9:1)
        "Who is this . . . ?"   (9:9)
        "Give ye them to eat"   (9:13)

5. Read 9:18-27. By comparing the four Gospels, we
learn that Luke does not record events which occurred
between 9:17 and 9:18. (See Chart C.) Instead he moves
ahead and focuses a bright light on this important conversation of Jesus with the twelve on the occasion of a special
prayer meeting.

Observe how Christ is the central Person of verses 18-22,
while disciples ("if any man") are the central ones of
verses 23-27.

Who Christ Is (9:18-22). Look at Chart D and recall that
the division 4:14—9:50 is called IDENTIFICATION.
Why was Jesus interested in how people identified Him?

_____

Observe Peter's precise reply. Account for Jesus' charge

of verse 21. What predictions are made in verse 22?_____

_____

Such *explicit* predictions of His coming death had not been
spoken by Jesus before this time. What is significant about

such a delay of revelation?_____

_____

Had the multitudes interpreted the Messianic prophecies to include death of the Messiah?_____.

_____

What Discipleship Is (9:23-27). Observe the emphasis on the voluntary, and on the "whosoever." What is true Christian discipleship?_____

_____

What glaring contrast of *values* appears in verse 25?_____

_____

What is suggested by the words "see the kingdom of God" (v. 27)?_____

_____

6. Read 9:28-50. The three paragraphs of this segment appear at first to be unrelated, but further study reveals some interesting connections.

The first paragraph (9:28-36) is a key paragraph in the gospel of Luke, recording the Father's recognition of His Son. It may be pointed out here that near each main junction of Luke's gospel, shown below, there is recorded an identification of Jesus.

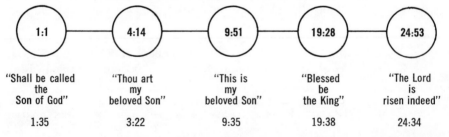

1:1	4:14	9:51	19:28	24:53
"Shall be called the Son of God"	"Thou art my beloved Son"	"This is my beloved Son"	"Blessed be the King"	"The Lord is risen indeed"
1:35	3:22	9:35	19:38	24:34

In the paragraph of 9:18-27, we studied men's identification of Jesus. Now, in 9:28-36, we read God's identification of Jesus.

What was Jesus engaged in when He experienced the transfiguration of verse 29?‡_____

_____

‡ Compare Jesus at prayer on other important occasions of His ministry: e.g., 3:21; 6:12; 9:18; 22:44.

Who appeared with Him; what aspect of Old Testament history did each represent; and what was the topic of their

conversation?_____

_____

What was Peter's presumption of verse 33, and how was it

rebuked? _____

_____

Observe the impact of verses 35*b* and 36*a*.
Compare the next paragraph (9:37-43*a*) with the transfiguration paragraph. Contrast "Look upon my son: for he is mine only child" (v. 38) and "This is my beloved Son: hear him" (v. 35). Compare verse 40 with verse 33. Also, contrast the apostles' impotency (v. 40) with their power

(9:1). How do you explain such a change?_____

_____

As you study the last paragraph (9:43*b*-50), observe especially these contrasts:
a. efficacious submission (v. 44), and false greatness (v. 46; cf. v. 33).
b. those against Jesus (v. 44), and those not against Him (vv. 49-50).
When did Jesus speak the words of verse 44 (see 43*b*)?___

_____

Explain verse 45._____

_____

Were the apostles expecting the earthly Messianic kingdom to be set up at this time? Does this account for the

discussion of verse 46?_____

_____

7.   As you think back over the passage of this lesson, write a list of five to ten important spiritual lessons which you have learned in your study. Include, among these, lessons

of Christian service, of the kind that Jesus was teaching
His apostles during their days of training._____

_____

_____

_____

_____

_____

III. NOTES.

1. Herd of pigs destroyed (8:33). The action of Jesus
was not unrighteous, unless Jesus Himself was unrighteous
and unjust. The gospel does not say who owned the swine;
divine judgment to their owner could have been for sins
entirely unrelated to the events of the narrative. Two posi-
tive benefits came of the destruction: people were reminded
of the worth of a man, and also heard about Jesus from the
healed man.

2. "I perceive that virtue is gone out of me" (8:46). The
word translated "virtue" means "power." This experience
of Jesus reveals that He was very conscious of active power
in His very being.

3. "The Son of man must suffer" (9:22). The word
"must" comes first in the Greek text, for emphasis. The
whole divine plan of redemption depended on the fulfillment of the prophesied substitutionary sacrifice. Christ *had*
to die if there was to be salvation for men.

4. "There be some standing here . . ." (9:27). Various
suggestions have been offered concerning the fulfillment of
this verse. One of the more common views is that the fulfillment was about a week later, in the transfiguration
(9:28 ff.), when some of the disciples were miraculously
given a brief view of one aspect of the coming kingdom.

IV. ADVANCED STUDY.

Three subjects out of this passage are recommended for
advanced study. For the last two, you may want to refer
especially to commentaries and a Bible encyclopedia.

1. The soils of the parable of the sower (8:4-15). Arrive at conclusions as to how hearts can be *prepared* to hear the Word of God, so that the seed will bring forth lasting fruit.
2. Jesus' use of parables in His teaching ministry. G. Campbell Morgan's book, *The Parables and Metaphors of Our Lord*, cited earlier, is an excellent study of this subject.
3. Demon possession: its causes, ill-effects and cure. Recommended outside reading: Merrill F. Unger's *Biblical Demonology*.§

V. CONCLUDING REMARKS.

Jesus was able to do what He did, and say what He said, because of *who He was*. Unless people rightly knew who He was, they would not understand the significance of His coming death. After Peter's words "You are the Christ of God," Jesus' quick response was, "I must be slain" (9:22, free trans.). Christ, the Son of God and Son of man, offered Himself to God in behalf of ungodly man. What matchless love!

§ Published Wheaton, Ill.: Van Kampen, 1952.

To Jerusalem

THE LIFE AND MINISTRY OF JESUS WERE

ALWAYS ACCORDING TO A PRECISE DIVINE

SCHEDULE FROM BEGINNING TO END.

He left heaven on time ("When the fulness of the time was come, God sent forth his Son," Gal. 4:4). And He returned to heaven on time. He knew just how long He was to continue His extended tour in Galilee (cf. Luke 4:18-19), before moving into the next and final phase culminating in His death, resurrection and ascension. For as Luke has recorded, "It came about, when the days were approaching for His ascension, that He resolutely set His face to go to Jerusalem" (Luke 9:51, NASB). The actual *hour* of death* would be about six months thence, after some final ministries in Judea, Perea, Samaria and Galilee, and with two visits to Jerusalem before the last one.†

With this lesson we begin the third main division of Luke's gospel (9:51 ff.). See Chart R for the context of the lesson.

We are calling this division "To Jerusalem" because, although Jesus continued to move back and forth for six months in the regions neighboring Jerusalem,‡ His eye was on one target event—the cross—and that would take place at the holy city.

The third division of Luke is also called "Instruction" on our survey chart. This is because the *word* ministry of Jesus is prominent at this time. Parables abound in this section. The arrangement is more topical than it is chronological. Also noteworthy is the fact that about 60 percent of the content of these chapters is found only in Luke. (All of chaps. 10 and 11 are peculiar to Luke.)

---

* Read Matt. 26:45; Mark 14:41; John 12:23.

† A comparison of Luke and John supports this chronology. Cf. John 7:2, 10, 37; 10:22-23. For a discussion of the difficult harmonistic problems involved, see A. T. Robertson, *A Harmony of the Gospels* (Nashville: Broadman, 1922), pp. 276-79.

‡ Cf. Luke 9:51; 13:22; 17:11.

1:1	4:14	9:51	19:28 24:53
PREPARATION	IDENTIFICATION	INSTRUCTION	SACRIFICE
	Galilee	To Jerusalem	At Jerusalem

	13:22
Later Judean Ministry	Perean Ministry

I. INITIAL OBSERVATIONS.

1. Mark the paragraph divisions in your Bible according to those shown on Chart S. Then read 9:51—11:54 paragraph by paragraph, underlining key words and phrases as you read, and making notes on items which you will want to examine more closely at a later time.

2. Record your paragraph titles on Chart S.

PARAGRAPH TITLES FOR 9:51—11:54

Chart S

			9:51 57 10:1 17 21 25 38 11:1 5	11:14 27 29 37 45	
TRAINING OF THE DISCIPLES				OPPOSITION AGAINST JEWS	
Service	Eternal Life	Communion		False and True Identifications of Jesus	Denunciations Against the Opposition

What groupings of paragraphs of similar content do you observe? Try to work out an outline of your own, and then compare it with the ones shown.

II. ANALYTICAL STUDY.

We will divide this analytical study into two parts, following the two sections on the chart: training (9:51—11:13), and opposition (11:14-54).

A. Training (9:51—11:13).

In the paragraphs of this section Jesus' training of the disciples, and of others, is prominent. Read each paragraph with this in mind, and record on Chart T the training involved. Also record what you feel is another main point of each paragraph.

JESUS' TRAINING OF THE DISCIPLES AND OTHERS   Chart T

Paragraph	Training	Other
9:51-56		
57-62		
10:1-16		
17-20		
21-24		
25-37		
38-42		
11:1-4		
5-13		

1. 9:51-56. Why would not the Samaritans extend hospitality to Jesus on His journey?_____

_____

What was Jesus' attitude toward such slight?_____

_____

What may we learn from this?_____

_____

2. 9:57-62. What is a key word of this paragraph?_____

_____

List all the things taught about discipleship here._____

_____

_____

3. 10:1-16. Observe the context of the familiar verse 2. What does this paragraph teach about the laborers, and about the harvest?_____

_____

Is an unresponding city (v. 10) considered part of the great harvest (v. 2)?_____

_____

4. 10:17-20. How are *service* and *salvation* compared in these verses?_____

_____

_____

5. 10:21-24. Why was Jesus rejoicing at this time?_____

_____

In view of the verses that follow, who are the "babes" of verse 21? _____

_____

Note the repetition of the words "Father" and "Son."

6. 10:25-37. In this paragraph Jesus is instructing a lawyer of the opposition group. What is the main lesson of this story of the good Samaritan?_____

What could the disciples have learned from this conversation, if they overheard it?_____

7. 10:38-42. Compare the words "many" (v. 41) and "one" (v. 42). Was Jesus rebuking Martha's labors, or her *overdoing* these things?_____
8. 11:1-4. In what sense was this a model prayer, to serve as a guide for us in our own individual praying?_____

Examine the prayer carefully, phrase by phrase. Observe the following: the One addressed; the order followed; the attitude of adoration and supplication; the kinds of petitions made, and about whom. James A. Frances has associated the following relationships with different phrases in the prayer. Write the phrase which is suggested by each:

child and his father:_____

worshiper and his God:_____

citizen and his king:_____

servant and his master:_____

beggar and his benefactor:_____

sinner and his Saviour:_____

pilgrim and his guide:_____

captive and his deliverer:_____

9. 11:5-13. What do these verses add to verses 1-4?_____

_____

What important lessons about prayer do you learn here?___

_____

_____

B. Opposition (11:14-54).

As you read these paragraphs, observe the kinds of accusations and challenges made by the people against Jesus. Write a list of the different things He said to them in rebuking their thoughts, words and deeds._____

_____

_____

_____

Have people changed in heart since Jesus' day?_____
1. 11:14-26. What is taught here about Satan and his

domain?_____

_____

2. 11:27-28. Compare this short paragraph with 8:19-21. How do the words "hear" and "keep" summarize man's

responsibility? _____

_____

3. 11:29-36. What sin is exposed here?_____

_____

How was Jesus greater than Jonah and Solomon? (Cf. Jonah 3:5 ff. and I Kings 10:1 ff.)_____

_____

How are verses 33-36 related to verses 29-32?_____

_____

4. 11:37-44. What various symptoms of hypocrisy appear

here? _____

_____

5. 11:45-54. The "lawyers" here were the teachers of the

law. How had they failed in their profession?_____

_____

III. NOTES.

1. "Suffer me first to go and bury my father" (9:59). Apparently the father was still living. The man was saying that he must take care of his father as long as his father was living. In view of this, interpret Jesus' words of verse 60.

2. "In that hour Jesus rejoiced in spirit" (10:21). The same Greek word (*pneuma*) can be translated "spirit" or "Spirit." Many versions (e.g., Berkeley, Good News for Modern Man, NASB, Williams) translate this verse to read "Holy Spirit."

3. "Thou art careful . . . about many things: but one thing is needful" (10:41-42). Of this Merrill C. Tenney writes, "Martha thought 'many things' were necessary for the Lord's comfort, and was wearing herself out to prepare them. Her company meant more to him than her cooking."§

4. Here is a good reading of 11:20: "No, it is rather by means of God's power that I drive out demons, which proves that the Kingdom of God has already come to you" (Good News for Modern Man).

5. "From the blood of Abel unto the blood of Zacharias" (11:51). Abel was the first Old Testament martyr (Gen. 4:8). Zacharias was the last martyr (II Chron. 24:20-22) in the Hebrew Bible, where Chronicles appears last in the list of books.

IV. ADVANCED STUDY.

1. Study the basic conflict between the "religion" of Pharisaism and the "life" of Christianity.

2. Pursue further your study of the harvest field, the laborers, and the Lord of the harvest (10:1-24). Compare such Scriptures as Jeremiah 3:15; Isaiah 6:8; Proverbs 11:30; Daniel 12:3; Mark 16:15, 20; Ephesians 4:11-12; I Corinthians 12:8-10; Colossians 1:29; Acts 16:6-7.

3. Further study of the Lord's prayer would also be very profitable. Compare the parallel passage in Matthew 6:9-13.

§ Charles F. Pfeiffer and Everett F. Harrison (eds.), *The Wycliffe Bible Commentary* (Chicago: Moody, 1962), p. 1047.

V.   CONCLUDING REMARKS.

When Jesus reached the last phase of His public ministry, and set His face to go to Jerusalem, those who pressed around Him were of two minds. Some were with Him, and for Him, like the disciple who said unto Him, "Lord, teach us to pray" (11:1). The others wished He were dead, like the scribes and Pharisees, who watched Him closely to trap Him in something He might say (11:54).

The bright and the dark—such were the hours of Jesus' experience. But He served in them all, seeking to save lost souls. This was the Son of man among men.

Through the Cities
and Villages, Teaching

JESUS' AUDIENCE CONTINUES TO ALTERNATE

BACK AND FORTH BETWEEN HIS FOLLOWERS

AND THE OPPOSITION IN THIS LESSON.

There are these major differences:

1. In 9:51—11:13 Jesus spoke mainly to the small groups of disciples (the twelve and the seventy). In the present lesson He speaks to all His followers, including those of the multitudes.

2. In 11:14-54 Jesus sharply denounced His enemies ("Woe unto you!"). In this lesson His tone is just as authoritative, but His words have more of a teaching content, appealing to the right as well as condemning the wrong.

If this lesson is studied in two parts, the second unit should begin at 13:22. The reasons for making a division at this point will be shown below.

I. INITIAL OBSERVATIONS.

The three chapters of this lesson are divided up into nineteen paragraphs, as shown on Chart U. As you read the text for first impressions, record paragraph titles in the spaces provided. Continue your study from there, following methods suggested in earlier lessons.

1. Justify the outlines shown on the chart by comparing the general contents of the paragraphs.

2. Read 13:22, comparing it with 9:51. Luke wants to remind his reader at this point, in the midst of much reporting of *words* of Jesus, that Jesus was still on His way to Jerusalem. Also, although the organization of 9:51—19:27 is mainly topical and only incidentally chronological and

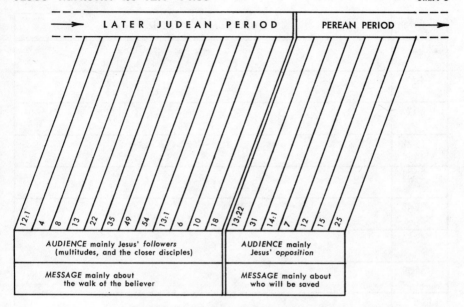

AUDIENCE mainly Jesus' followers (multitudes, and the closer disciples)	AUDIENCE mainly Jesus' opposition
MESSAGE mainly about the walk of the believer	MESSAGE mainly about who will be saved

geographical, Luke has inserted 13:22 to recognize the beginning of Jesus' three-month Perean ministry.*

3. Record where parables and healings appear. Keep in mind that parables abound in the *Instruction* section of Luke.

4. Identify the audience of 12:1—13:21 more explicitly by noting such verses as 12:1, 4, 13, 22, 32, 41, 54; 13:10.

II. ANALYTICAL STUDY.

A. 12:1—13:21.

Study 12:1—13:21 to learn all that Jesus taught about the walk of the believer. Record your findings for each paragraph on Chart V.

1. What paragraphs talk about the coming of Christ?___

---

* Perea is the region on the east side of the southern half of the Jordan River. (Cf. John 10:39-42.) See Irving L. Jensen, *Studies in the Life of Christ* (Chicago: Moody, 1969), for the geography and chronology of these months.

Paragraph	WALK OF A BELIEVER
12:1-3	
4-7	
8-12	
13-21	
22-34	
35-48	
49-53	
54-59	
13:1-5	
6-9	
10-17	
18-21	

Compare what is said about the *day* and *hour* of His coming (12:40, 46) with that of the *time* of His coming (12:54-57). _____

What should be the believer's attitude with respect to both situations? _____

2. Here is a modern speech reading of 12:49-50: "I have come to cast fire on the earth, and how I wish it were already kindled! I have an overwhelming baptism to undergo and how strained I feel until it is finished!" (Berkeley). Interpret the rest of the paragraph in light of these verses.

B.   13:22—14:35.

Read through this section paragraph by paragraph, and record on Chart W what is said about salvation and the saved ones. Most of the teaching here is by parable or illustration. In a parable look especially for the one *main* truth.

PEREAN PERIOD   Chart W

Paragraph	SALVATION AND THE SAVED ONES
13:22-30	
31-35	
14:1-6	
7-11	
12-14	
15-24	
25-35	

1.   What essentially was Jesus' answer to the question of 13:23, "Are there few that be saved?" (Consider vv. 28-29 in answering this.) _____

_____

2.   Read 13:32-33 in a modern version. Compare the tones and teachings of each of these verses:

Verse	Tone	Teaching
32		
33		
34		
35		

Meditate long over verse 34. What is revealed about the heart of Christ here?_____

_____

3. What spiritual truth is illustrated by the phrase "fallen into a pit" (14:5)?_____

4. What are the lessons about discipleship taught in 14:25-35? _____

_____

Read 14:26 in other versions for the intended meaning of "hate."

5. What verses of this lesson do you consider to be key verses? _____

_____

_____

III. NOTES.

1. "Blasphemeth against the Holy Ghost" (12:10). Jesus continues to call and invite men to Himself, even while they reject Him. Blasphemy and resistance against the Holy Spirit immobilize the Spirit in His convicting and enlightening ministry of leading to Christ; and as long as He is so resisted, forgiveness is wanting.

2. "Division" (12:51). Because salvation is an individual matter, divisions in families appear when some members choose to follow Christ, and the others refuse to do so. This is true in all families, but especially so in the strongly knit Jewish home, even to this day.

3. "The Galileans, whose blood Pilate had mingled" (13:1). The fanatical nationalists had apparently created a disturbance in Jerusalem's temple area. The Siloam tower catastrophe was another recent incident that caused people to discuss the subject of divine judgment.

IV. ADVANCED STUDY.

Make a study of the kingdom of God, as this subject is taught by the Gospels. The phrase "kingdom of heaven" should also be considered in such a study. Concordance, encyclopedia, harmony of the Gospels and commentary are the four main outside helps for the project. Answer such questions as What? When? Where? and Who?

V. CONCLUDING REMARKS.

Jesus was very much aware of His approaching death, but He always looked beyond death to the resurrection and coronation. This is why He kept speaking of His next coming.

"The Son of man cometh at an hour when ye think not" (12:40).

"Ye shall not see me, until the time come when ye shall say, Blessed is he that cometh in the name of the Lord" (13:35).

Sixty years later the Apostle John concluded his inspired volume with the prayer "Even so, come, Lord Jesus" (Rev. 22:20).

Are we watching for His coming?

Six Parables

OF THE DIFFERENT GROUPS OF PARABLES

RECORDED IN THE GOSPELS, NONE IS MORE

FAMILIAR THAN THE ONE IN CHAPTER 15.

It is the parable of the lost sheep, the lost coin and the lost son. Immediately following these parables Luke records three others, on stewardship. The six parables and the context surrounding them are the subject of our present lesson. We recall from our previous studies that this is the period of Jesus' public ministry where parables abound.

I. INITIAL OBSERVATIONS.

1. In your first reading of 15:1—17:10, look for the following:
   a. to whom Jesus is speaking
   b. key words and phrases

GOD'S GRACE AND MAN'S RESPONSIBILITIES Chart X

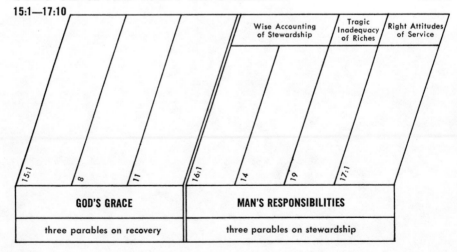

15:1—17:10

| | | | | Wise Accounting of Stewardship | Tragic Inadequacy of Riches | Right Attitudes of Service |

15:1 · 8 · 11 · 16:1 · 14 · 19 · 17:1

| GOD'S GRACE | MAN'S RESPONSIBILITIES |
| three parables on recovery | three parables on stewardship |

2. Keeping in mind that great multitudes (14:25) heard Jesus speak the words of 14:26-35, relate 15:1 (especially the word "hear") to 14:35b.

3. Our present unit of study goes through 17:10. Read 17:11, noting the geographical references. That verse begins the unit of our next lesson.

4. Paragraph titles (record these on Chart X)

Study the outlines shown on the chart, and compare them with your own observations of the common content of groups of paragraphs.

II. ANALYTICAL STUDY.

A. God's Grace (Three Parables on Recovery) 15:1-32.

Jesus spoke these three parables (sometimes called *one* parable of three parts) to answer the accusation of 15:2. Read this verse, and keep it in mind as you interpret the parables.

Compare the three parables, looking for the things that are alike, and things that are not alike. Record these. *Things that are alike:*

_____

_____

_____

_____

Things that are not alike:

Aspect	Lost Sheep	Lost Coin	Lost Son

1. Do the parables teach *mainly* the same truth? If so, what is it?_____

_____

2. Does 15:7 ignore the necessity of righteous living?___

_____

3. Compare the phrase "I have found" (15:6, 9) with "he came to himself" (15:17)._____
Did God have anything to do with the prodigal's soul-searching? _____

_____

4. Compare "give me" (15:12) with "make me" (15:19).

_____

_____

5. Compare the younger son's sin of riotous living (v. 13) with that of the elder son's sin of anger (v. 28)._____

_____

Were both in need of the father's help?_____

_____

6. What do these parables teach about God and about sinful man?_____

_____

_____

**B. Man's Responsibilities (Three Parables on Steward-
ship) 16:1—17:10.**

1. Wise Accounting of Stewardship. Read 16:1-18.
Note the phrase "There was a certain rich man" (16:1).
Compare this with 15:11 and 16:19. These were parables very likely based on actual situations.

Does Jesus condone dishonesty in this parable?_____
As you study the parable, look for its *main* teaching. What

did Jesus teach in verses 8-9?_____

Read verse 9*a* as, "Make friends for yourselves with worldly wealth" (Good News for Modern Man).

Is money itself evil?_____
How can a wise and generous sharing of money be beneficial to the Christian so sharing?_____

What important truths appear in verses 10-13?_____

How is verse 14 related to what goes before?_____

How are verses 15-18 directed to the evils of Pharisaism?

2. Tragic Inadequacy of Riches. Read 16:19-31.
Is anything said here about the spiritual condition of the rich man and of the beggar?_____
From their two destinies after death, what may be concluded concerning this?_____

What is the *main* point of this parable?_____

What additional truth is taught by verse 31?_____

3. Right Attitudes of Service. Read 17:1-10.
Record below one right attitude of service taught by these verses:

1-2: _____

3-4: _____

5-6: _____

7-10: _____

4. Think back over the passage you have been studying for this lesson, and summarize the main spiritual truths taught about God's grace and man's responsibilities._____

_____

_____

_____

_____

III. NOTES.

1. "Make to yourselves friends of [literally, 'by means of'] the mammon of unrighteousness" (16:9). The phrase "mammon of unrighteousness" was Jesus' epithet for "money." Herbert Lockyer writes,

> The possession of weath, influence, position, leisure, or opportunity are so to be used here on earth as never to be forgotten in the eternal state . . . . Our choice is between two motives— love of possessions for their own sake . . . or the use of possessions as a trust from God for the benefit of others, and for the glory of the Giver of all good gifts.*

2. "And in hell he lift up his eyes" (16:23). This hell (Greek, *Hades*) is not the eternal state of suffering, but the woeful abode of departed spirits between death and the resurrection. The Old Testament Hebrew word for the same place is *Sheol*. Lazarus was in "Abraham's bosom," the happy abode of deceased saints during those times.

IV. ADVANCED STUDY.

Make a study of the intermediate state—between death and resurrection—of believers and unbelievers. Distinguish between Old and New Testament times. Your study

---

* Herbert Lockyer, *All the Parables of the Bible* (Grand Rapids: Zondervan, 1963), p. 291.

will center about such words as hell, Hades, Sheol, paradise. Use a Bible concordance, dictionary, encyclopedia and book of doctrines for your sources.

V. CONCLUDING REMARKS.

In His public ministry Jesus spoke about many things to His disciples and to the multitudes. Of the many things He said, He seemed to be happiest when He could talk about the conversion of a soul. This is why He is in His glory in Luke 15. An exclamation point could rightly be placed at the end of the last verse: "It was meet that we should make merry, and be glad: for this thy brother was dead, and is alive again; and was lost, and is found!"

LESSON 10   Luke 17:11—19:27

Kingdom Teaching

THIS LESSON COVERS JESUS' LAST WORDS

AND WORKS BEFORE HE REACHED JERUSALEM

FOR THE WEEK OF SACRIFICE AND TRIUMPH.

Typical of Luke in the Instruction section (9:51—19:27), chronology and geography are not prominent in the passage of this lesson, because Luke is emphasizing the *content* of Jesus' ministry (especially His words). A comparative study of the Gospels places 17:11—19:27 in the geographical outline shown on Chart Y.

GEOGRAPHICAL OUTLINE   **Chart Y**
17:11—19:27

TO PEREA	THROUGH PEREA	TO BETHANY
Luke 17:11—18:14	Luke 18:15-34	Luke 18:35—19:27
	cf. Matthew 19:1—20:28; Mark 10:1-45	cf. Matthew 20:29-34; Mark 10:46; 14:3-9; John 11:55—12:11

I.   INITIAL OBSERVATIONS.

1.   Note that the verse 17:11 is devoted entirely to geography. In Luke's gospel such a verse is a divisional point in the narrative (cf. 4:14; 9:51; 13:22; 19:28-29). Note on Chart Z how 17:11 begins a new section of Jesus' Perean ministry.

2.   Before reading 17:11—19:27, mark in your Bible this geographical outline:

78

Part One	Interruption	Part Two
Luke 13:22—17:10	LAZARUS EVENT John 11:1-54	Luke 17:11—19:27

To Perea* (17:11 ff.)
Through Perea† (18:15 ff.)
To Bethany (18:35 ff.; cf. 19:29)

Observe the geographical references in the following verses of Luke: 18:31, 35; 19:1, 11.

3. As you read the passage for initial observations, note the different groups to whom Jesus spoke; the parables He taught; and the healings He performed.

II. ANALYTICAL STUDY.

One of the important subjects of Jesus' teaching was that of the kingdom. Jesus knew, as the prophets had taught, that in the end times He would be sitting on the Davidic throne. That was the kingdom especially oriented to Israel, according to covenant promises. But Jesus had in mind now a *larger* kingdom, as large and universal as the gospel itself, existing right now ("the kingdom of God *is* within you," 17:21).

If you made an advanced study of the kingdom in Lesson 8, you may have considered such subjects as: citizens of the kingdom; conduct of the citizens; the King and the commencement of His reign; blessings of the kingdom. Multitudes of Jesus' contemporaries had false views about the kingdom, hence His instruction concerning it.

Study the paragraphs of this passage to learn what Jesus

---

* The Berkeley Version reads 17:11*b* thus: "He crossed between Samaria and Galilee." *The Wycliffe Bible Commentary* says, "He followed the border between the two provinces across the Jordan, and down the east side of the river; for the next place mentioned is Jericho (19:1), the point at which pilgrims usually returned to the west side" (Chicago: Moody, 1962), p. 1056.

† In order to understand the reason for this geographical reference, compare Luke 18:15 with Matt. 19:1, 13 and Mark 10:1, 13.

was teaching (whether by word or works) about the present kingdom. Record your conclusions below. (Note: It is not necessary to find the word "kingdom" in a paragraph to classify its verses as kingdom instruction. Have in mind the large kingdom of the gospel as you read. The phrases supplied below, with each paragraph, suggest lines of study.)

Paragraph	The Kingdom of the Gospel
17:11-19	Objects of mercy
20-37	Time of the kingdom
18:1-8	Faith
9-14	Contriteness
15-17	Entrance into the kingdom
18-30	Surrender
31-34	The King
35-43	Son of David
19:1-10	Potential citizens
11-27	Stewardship

After you have completed this study, go back over the paragraphs again, observing other important truths taught in this passage. For example:

a. What is the common need expressed in the two healing

incidents (17:11-19; 18:35-43)?_____

_____

Note the gratitude in both instances.

b. What is taught about the second coming of Christ?

_____

_____

c. What is taught about prayer?_____

_____

d. What is taught about stewardship?_____

_____

III. NOTES.

1. "The kingdom of God is within [or 'among'] you" (17:21). Jesus, who was standing among the people, had brought the kingdom with Him. In that sense the kingdom was among them.

2. "They did eat, they drank,‡ they married . . ." (17:27; cf. v. 28). The activities referred to here were harmless in themselves. Preoccupation with them, in a mood of materialism, had brought a neglect and rejection of God's message. Such is the description of the times when Jesus shall come again.

3. "None is good, save one, that is, God" (18:19). Jesus was not disclaiming His deity here. The ruler had used a complimentary title "Good Master." Did he really mean *good* in its ultimate sense? We can imagine Jesus saying here, in effect, "You know that only God is truly good. And are you genuinely recognizing Me as having *such* a divine attribute?"

4. "How hardly shall they that have riches enter . . ." (18:24). "How hardly" here means "with what difficulty." The illustration of camel and needle (v. 25) is a hyperbole,

_____

‡ The combination "did eat . . . drank" has an amoral connotation.

suggesting something impossible. But, "the things which are impossible with men are possible with God" (v. 27).

IV. ADVANCED STUDY.

Miracles played an important part in Jesus' ministry. Refer to a Bible dictionary or encyclopedia§ for a discussion of this vital subject. Some of the topics to consider when studying the miracles of Jesus are these: kinds, methods, purposes, importance, effects. What do the miracles of this lesson teach concerning any of these topics? What is God's designed program of miracles today?

V. CONCLUDING REMARKS.

"All things that are written by the prophets concerning the Son of man shall be accomplished" (18:31). Jesus' consciousness of His Messianic mission, and the exact fulfillment of the prophets' predictions, are two of the strongest witnesses of the divine origin of Christianity.

§ E.g., James Orr (ed.), *The International Standard Bible Encyclopedia*, III (Grand Rapids: Eerdmans, 1952), pp. 2062-66; and Merrill F. Unger, *Unger's Bible Dictionary* (Chicago: Moody, 1957), pp. 747-50.

Last Messages

SIX MONTHS EARLIER JESUS HAD SET HIS

FACE TO GO TO JERUSALEM TO DIE; NOW

THE TIME HAD COME FOR THIS RENDEZVOUS.

There were six more days of life for Him, before the cross. For three days (Sunday through Tuesday) He would speak to the multitudes in the public places. (This is the subject of our present lesson.) He would spend two quiet days (Wednesday and Thursday) mainly with His disciples. On Friday, the violent day, He would be scourged and crucified. Study Chart AA to have fixed in your mind this sequence of Passion Week.

PASSION WEEK   Chart AA

King Extolled   King Mocked

Ministry to the Public			Ministry to the Disciples		Solitary Ministry
Sunday	Monday	Tuesday	Wednesday	Thursday	Friday
Luke 19:28—21:38			°	22:7-38	22:39—23:56
Active Days			Quiet Days		Violent Day
AUTHORITY			COMPASSION		SUBMISSION
Jesus speaks much					Jesus speaks little

° None of the Gospels records events for Wednesday.

As mentioned above, this lesson is about the first three days of the Passion Week. During this time Jesus ministered mostly in speaking (cf. 19:47; 20:1). These were His last messages before the cross. Keep this in mind as you study this lesson.

I. INITIAL OBSERVATIONS.

This passage of Luke may be divided into three parts, shown below:

Entry into Jerusalem	19:28-44	Compassion of Jesus
Confrontation in Jerusalem	19:45—21:4	Authority of Jesus
Prophecy about Jerusalem	21:5-36	Foreknowledge of Jesus

(Conclusion: 21:37-38)

Read the entire passage in one sitting with the above outline in mind. Also, as you read, underline key words and phrases for later study, and record some of your initial impressions.

II. ANALYTICAL STUDY.

We will divide our analytical study into three units, according to the above outline.

A. Entry into Jerusalem (19:28-44; new paragraphs at vv. 28, 36, 41).

For this segment record your observations on an analytical chart, similar to Chart BB. Use the space inside the boxes for writing the biblical text, and the margins for recording your observations and outlines.

1. Read 19:28-35. Ponder the significant fact that *the Lord needed a colt*. Relate the colt and stones (v. 40) to the glory of God in this context.

What miraculous elements appear in this paragraph?_____

(1) Dependent on a Colt

28

Ascending up to Jerusalem

. . . the Lord hath need of him

Ye shall find   Colt

And they found

(2) Praised as a King

36

Multitude rejoicing

Blessed be the king

Glory

Pharisees

— the STONES would . . . cry out

Pharisees objecting

Stones

(3) Grieved for Lost Souls

41

— he beheld

— and WEPT over it

TEARS

TRIBULATION

44

2. Read 19:36-40. What are the contrasting atmospheres of this paragraph?_____

Note the emphatic phrases of verses 37-38 (cf. Ps. 118:25-26). Account for the Pharisees' objection._____

3. Read 19:41-44. Why did Jesus weep over the city?___

Read verses 42 and 44 in modern versions to learn more clearly what Jesus meant by these words. What attributes of Jesus are disclosed in this paragraph?_____

B. Confrontation in Jerusalem (19:45—21:4; new paragraphs at 19:45; 20:1, 9, 20, 27, 41; 21:1).

This is a passage of conflict between the old order, represented by the religious leaders of the masses, and the new order, represented by Jesus. Read the passage paragraph by paragraph, observing the main point of each. Note specific references to Jesus' teaching and preaching (cf. 21:37). In what paragraphs does the opposition initiate conversation? _____

Where does Jesus open the discussion?_____

Make a study of the old order and the new. Record your observations on the accompanying chart.

C. Prophecy About Jerusalem (21:5-36; new paragraphs at vv. 5, 20, 25, 34).

This prophecy of Jesus, known as the Olivet Discourse, is an expansion of the theme of 19:43-44. Matthew 24—25

Paragraph Reference and Title	Old Order Versus the New Order	
	Words and Actions of the Opposition	Words and Actions of Jesus
19:45-48		
20:1-8		
20:9-19		
20:20-26		
20:27-40		
20:41-47		
21:1-4		

and Mark 13 report the same discourse. Jerusalem, holy city of the Jews, is the focal point of the prophecies. Before studying the passage, the following items should be recognized:

1. THIS IS A PROPHECY OF DOUBLE PERSPECTIVE. Jesus was predicting (1) the siege and fall of Jerusalem, which took place when the Romans under Vespasian and Titus conquered the city in A.D. 70; (2) the tribulation times before the second coming of Christ (cf. 21:27, 31). (Some interpret both prophecies to be intended throughout the discourse. Another view says the fall of Jerusalem is prophesied in vv. 8-24, and the end times prophesied in vv. 25-36.)

2. THE NATION OF ISRAEL, PARTICULARLY, IS IN VIEW HERE. Read verse 24 for support of this. This verse teaches a worldwide dispersion of the Jews "until the times of the Gentiles be fulfilled," which is in the last days.

3. "THIS GENERATION" OF VERSE 32 REFERRED TO EITHER THE PEOPLE LIVING WHEN JESUS SPOKE THE WORDS, OR TO ISRAEL AS A NATION. In view of such verses as 21:27, which is still future, the latter interpretation is more sure.

4. THE PRACTICAL VALUE OF THIS DISCOURSE FOR US
TODAY IS TWOFOLD.
   a. The fulfillment of the prophecies in A.D. 70 confirms
      again the truth of Jesus' words.
   b. The warnings and exhortations given throughout the
      discourse are of much help for believers, who should
      always be living in expectation of the Lord's coming.

An exhaustive study of the Olivet Discourse requires a
comparison of the texts of Matthew, Mark and Luke, but
that is beyond the scope of this study manual. The following exercise is a practical one and should be pursued with
utmost diligence because Jesus' words are so timely.

Look mainly for three kinds of truths spoken by Jesus:
description of tribulation, assurance of deliverance, and
exhortation for conduct. Continually apply these with reference to Christ's return to this earth. Record your observations below.

Paragraph	Tribulation	Deliverance	Exhortation
21:5-19			
20-24			
25-33			
34-36			

III. NOTES.

1. The Sadducees (20:27). They were not as numerous as the Pharisees, nor as outspoken against Jesus' teaching. This is partly because they were more interested in politics than in theological questions. The chief priests, most of whom were Sadducees, actively opposed Jesus in His trial and crucifixion, perhaps mostly out of a fear that His Messianic movement would bring political ruin. Sadducees denied the existence of angels, spirits, and life after death (cf. Acts 23:8).

2. "Times of the Gentiles" (21:24). This phase refers to an era of Gentile supremacy in world politics. The era began with the year of Judah's Babylonian captivity under Nebuchadnezzar (586 B.C.) and will close at the second coming of Christ. Then follows Israel's restoration to favor.

IV. ADVANCED STUDY.

1. Make a comparative study of the three Gospels reporting the Olivet Discourse. You will probably want to consult various commentaries for help in interpretation.
2. Another interesting study concerns Jesus' use of questions in His conversations with people. Examine His questions of this passage and derive some valuable lessons.
3. Jesus is Prophet, Priest and King. Observe that these offices generally relate to the past, present and future, respectively. Study the subject of Jesus' kingship. Compare such passages as Matthew 2:2; Luke 19:38; 23:38; Revelation 19:11-16.
4. Another suggested topic of study is the authority of Jesus (Luke 20:2). Use the following passages for your study: John 1:1, 14; 11:43-44; I Timothy 3:16; Luke 4:18; 7:11-15; 8:26-33; 8:52-55; Matthew 4:10-11; Luke 22:69; Acts 7:55; Philippians 2:9-11; Romans 14:9; Hebrews 1:8; Ephesians 1:20-21; Daniel 7:14; Revelation 19:13, 16.

V. CONCLUDING REMARKS.

"Heaven and earth shall pass away; but *my words* shall not pass away" (21:33). Jesus' words were not only true and authoritative; they were of *eternal* import. With eternity in view, then, we should listen to Him as He reveals the Father, accredits the Scriptures, describes His mission, invites sinners to be saved, and prophesies of things to come.

"All the people came early in the morning to him in the temple, for to *hear him*" (21:38). Are we earnest listeners today?

The Great Sacrifice

WE HAVE STUDIED JESUS' PASSION WEEK

MESSAGES, DELIVERED IN JERUSALEM'S

PUBLIC PLACES, ESPECIALLY THE TEMPLE AREA.

Those were the early days of the week when the religious leaders had not yet stirred up the mobs to the point of murderous intent. Recall 21:38, where Luke reports that Jesus had a large following of inquirers among the multitude who "came early in the morning . . . to hear him." There must have been many who accepted His message as true.

Now at 22:1 Luke begins the darkest chapters of Jesus' life. He tells of the satanic plot to betray Jesus (22:1-6); the sad last hours of Jesus with His disciples (22:7-46); the cruel scorn hurled against Him by the religious rulers and the mobs they incited (22:47—23:25); the agony of scourging and crucifixion (23:26-56).

It is not our purpose in these lessons to compare all four Gospels to gather the *full* story of Jesus' passion. Such a study is devoted to the topic generally known as "The Life of Christ." Our purpose now is to learn from the material which Luke, inspired by the Holy Spirit, has chosen to include as his text. Luke writes about *the Son of man among men.* We will be observing in this lesson how the Son of man was accused and slain by the men among whom He walked.

I.   INITIAL OBSERVATIONS.

This passage may be divided into nineteen paragraphs. You are probably aware by now in your study of Luke's gospel that chapter divisions aren't always indicative of major junctions in the narrative. The paragraphical meth-

91

od of study is a very profitable way to approach the text of a Bible passage.

Note the paragraph divisions of Chart CC. Mark these divisions in your Bible. Then read 22:1—23:56 at one time, paragraph by paragraph. Follow study procedures suggested in earlier lessons, including recording paragraph titles on the chart.

EVENTS OF THURSDAY AND FRIDAY   Chart CC
22:1—23:56

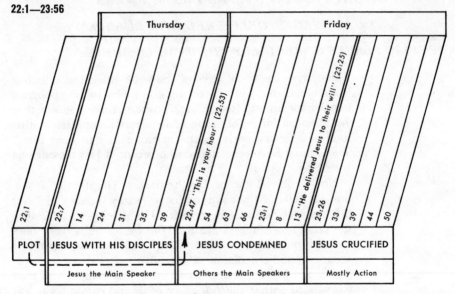

1. Note how the first paragraph (22:1-6) introduces this entire section. Where in the narrative does Judas next appear? What happens in the meantime?_____

_____

2. Observe the significant phrases of 22:53 and 23:25, shown on the chart. Explain "your hour" and "their will" in view of the sovereignty of God._____

_____

_____

3. Study the outlines on the chart, observing how your paragraph titles fit into each group.

4. Try making an outline of your own, looking for *groups* of common content in the paragraphs.

II. ANALYTICAL STUDY.

Various methods of analysis have been suggested in the lessons of this study guide. As you analyze the passage of this lesson, use any of these methods, or an adaptation of them. Some important rules to remember in *all* Bible analysis are these:
1. Observe carefully. Look, and keep on looking!
2. Record your observations. Jot them down!
3. Be orderly in your procedures. This suggests also that you aim for organized outlines whenever possible.

The study questions given in the next pages are designed to help you find the important truths of the text. Don't forget to *apply* the text at all times.

A. Plot (22:1-6).

1. Note the reference to the Passover feast. Picture the mass influx of people into Jerusalem at this time, from near and far.

2. Account for the religious leaders' fear of the people (22:2, 6). Compare 21:38._____

_____

3. Explain "Then entered Satan into Judas" (22:3).___

_____

_____

B. Jesus with His Disciples (22:7-46).

1. Read 22:7-23. Make a note of the various predictions of Jesus in these verses. The communion service (Lord's Table) of the church today originated in this event. What

is symbolized by the cup and by the bread?_____

_____

What is the main purpose of the Lord's Table (v. 19)?___

_____

2. Read 22:24-30. Compare the strife of verse 24 with the discussion of verse 23. What does Jesus teach about greatness here? _____

3. Read 22:31-34. Translate "you" of verse 31 as plural: "all of you." What is taught here about the believer's frailty, Satan's interest, and the Lord's help?_____

_____

_____

4. Read 22:35-38. Observe the key phrase "But now" (v. 36). How was this approaching hour different, both for Jesus and for His disciples, from the previous time?___

Note that Jesus advised that each disciple buy a sword. Do you see a parable in this advice? In answering this, keep in mind the two swords of verse 38, and Jesus' remark "It is enough." What do you think Jesus meant by this latter phrase?_____

5. Read 22:39-46. The human nature of Jesus is prominent in this paragraph. List the things taught here about that nature. _____

_____

_____

How was Jesus' will related to His Father's?_____

_____

What do you learn about prayer from these verses?_____

_____

_____

_____

C. Jesus Condemned (22:47—23:25).

Jesus rose up from prayer (22:45) when He knew that the enemy's hour had arrived (22:53). In His confidence of victory He could face His enemy without flinching. Some wonderful examples of triumph through trial are seen in the next paragraphs of Luke.

1. Read 22:47-53. Account for the miracle (v. 51) being

performed at this time._____

_____

How would such a miracle enforce Jesus' words of verses

52 and 53?_____

_____

2. Read 22:54-62. Peter is the key character of this paragraph. Study the sequence reported, noting where he was, what he said, and what he did. What are the important

spiritual lessons?_____

_____

_____

3. Read 22:63—23:12. In these four paragraphs Jesus appears before individuals and groups to be questioned and scorned. Make a comparative study of the questions

asked Jesus, and His replies._____

_____

_____

_____

4. Read 23:13-25. Who were the leaders inciting the

mobs to demand Jesus' death?_____

_____

What basically was Pilate's reason for delivering Jesus to the will of the people?_____

D. Jesus Crucified (23:26-56).

Luke has condensed into these five short paragraphs a moving story of the events associated with Jesus' crucifixion. In your analysis of the paragraphs, study especially the words of Jesus, and the words of people. Record in the spaces below what you consider to be the highlights of each paragraph.

LAMENTATION (vv. 26-32)

MOCKERY (vv. 33-38)

REPENTANCE (vv. 39-43)

COMMITTAL (vv. 44-49)

DEVOTION (vv. 50-56)

As you think back over the passage of this lesson, what are the impressions that linger with you?_____

_____

_____

Do you feel that you know Jesus more intimately? Has this renewed insight into the sacrifice of God's Son for your sins deepened your gratitude to God?

III. NOTES.

1. "Sit on thrones judging the twelve tribes of Israel" (22:30). Jesus here clearly taught that Israel as a nation had a future history. This would be in the "New Age" (Matt. 19:28, Berkeley and Good News for Modern Man).

2. "Here are two swords" (22:38). Lange's commentary calls this remark by the disciples and Jesus' reply, "It is enough," a "melancholy irony." "Two swords over against the whole might of the world, of hell, and of death, which were to engage in the assault upon Him!"*

3. "Council" (22:66). The Greek word is *synēdrion*, from which comes the name Sanhedrin (as in the Berkeley Version). The Sanhedrin was the highest Jewish tribunal in a Jewish city, exercising civil jurisdiction according to Mosaic Law, and a restricted measure of criminal jurisdiction. Its seventy (or seventy-two) members came from three groups: chief priests, scribes and elders.

4. Pilate (23:1) and Herod (23:8). Pontius Pilate was the Roman governor (procurator) of Palestine from A.D. 26 to 36. The Herod mentioned in the story was Herod Antipas, tetrarch of the regions of Galilee and Perea. Pilate referred Jesus to Herod when he learned that Jesus was a Galilean (23:7).

IV. ADVANCED STUDY.

1. A very fruitful method of Bible study is the biographical method. We can learn much from people in the Bible because they, like us, were human. We can learn from their talk and from their walk, whether good or bad, and, if we are wise, we will steer our lives accordingly.

Study each of the following persons, using the information Luke gives concerning them. Record all your findings, and make a list of practical lessons learned.

Judas

Peter

Pilate

Herod

Malefactors

Joseph

---

* John Peter Lange, *Commentary on the Holy Scriptures, Luke* (Grand Rapids: Zondervan reprint, n.d.), p. 343.

2.   Study the subject of suffering and trial. No one has experienced deeper anguish of soul than did Jesus during this Passion Week. Even words of Scripture, because they are of human language, cannot fully reveal the agony of His spirit in Gethsemane (22:44), and the physical tortures of scourging (John 19:1) and crucifixion (Luke 23:33).

In your study of suffering, arrive at answers to such questions as:

Why did Jesus have to suffer?

Why do the righteous suffer today?

What strength and comfort is given the Christian to bolster him in the hour of trial?

For verses on the subject of suffering, consult a concordance under such words as "trial," "affliction" and "suffering." Include in your study Matthew 16:24; Acts 9:16; II Timothy 3:12; Philippians 1:29; I Peter 1:11; 2:20-21; Hebrews 2:9; 12:5-11; Romans 8:17-18.

3.   Compare the three crosses of 23:39-43. How are the two malefactors representative of the two segments of mankind? According to these verses, what is the way of salvation?

V.   CONCLUDING REMARKS.

"It was about twelve o'clock when the sun stopped shining" (23:44, Good News for Modern Man). So crucial was the death of Jesus as far as mankind's destiny was concerned that God's nature itself bowed in awe with signs and wonders. What solemn hours were these, as the Son gave His spirit to His Father, for the world!

The Grand Miracle

THE TONE OF PRAISE AND BLESSING WHICH

PERVADES THE FIRST CHAPTER OF LUKE

REAPPEARS NOW AT THE LAST CHAPTER.

From the chamber of the empty tomb echoes forth in matchless glory the triumphant message "He is not here, but is risen" (24:6). When Luke wrote his narrative, about thirty years had transpired since Jesus' resurrection; but the glory of the event had not subsided. Read the last four verses of Luke's gospel and you will be convinced that intense joy must have filled his heart as he laid down his pen on completion of his writing task. Could any book close on a more triumphant note?

I. INITIAL OBSERVATIONS.

Chapter 24 is of three parts: vv. 1-12; vv. 13-35; vv. 36-53. Read the chapter once or twice for first impressions. Be sure to mark key words and phrases in your Bible for later study.

Note every instance when a description is given of the hearts of Jesus' followers (e.g., "perplexed," v. 4).

Chart DD is a work sheet for comparing the three segments of the chapter. Study the surveys shown, and add your own observations. This is good preparation for analytical studies that follow.

Study carefully the outline which shows what brought on *recognition, assurance* and *praise*. Find support for this study in the biblical text.

II. ANALYTICAL STUDY.

Read each segment carefully before answering the questions.

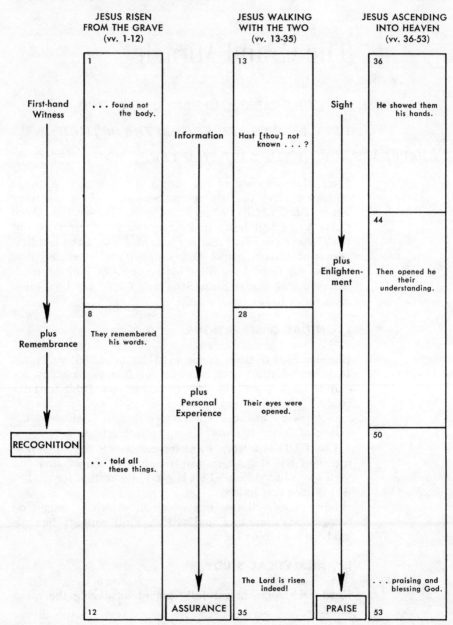

JESUS RISEN
FROM THE GRAVE
(vv. 1-12)

JESUS WALKING
WITH THE TWO
(vv. 13-35)

JESUS ASCENDING
INTO HEAVEN
(vv. 36-53)

First-hand
Witness

. . . found not
the body.

Information

Hast [thou] not
known . . . ?

Sight

He showed them
his hands.

plus
Enlighten-
ment

Then opened he
their
understanding.

plus
Remembrance

They remembered
his words.

plus
Personal
Experience

Their eyes were
opened.

RECOGNITION

. . . told all
these things.

ASSURANCE

The Lord is risen
indeed!

PRAISE

. . . praising and
blessing God.

A. Jesus Risen from the Grave (24:1-12).

1. What were the women's reactions after seeing the empty tomb?_____

_____

What may have been going through their minds?_____

_____

_____

2. Analyze the words of the angels:
question (v. 5):
statement of fact (v. 6*a*):
reminder of command (v. 6*b*):
3. Is there any suggestion from verses 8 and 9, that the women had begun to believe the resurrection fact?_____

_____

Compare the reactions of the other disciples (v. 11) and Peter (v. 12) with the women's._____

_____

B. Jesus Walking with the Two Disciples (24:13-35).

1. Compare verses 16 and 31. Was there a divine purpose in keeping the disciples from recognizing Jesus at this time? If so, what may it have been?_____

_____

2. What does verse 21*a* reveal about the disciples' concept of Messiahship?_____

_____

3. Study carefully verses 25-27. What was the basis for Jesus' rebuke? _____

_____

What place did He give the Scriptures, as related to a man's life?_____

_____

How did He relate the Old Testament to His own ministry?

_____

_____

4.   What is the significance of the action of verse 30 in view of the fact that Jesus was a Guest, not the host? Compare verse 35._____

_____

5.   What are the miracles of verse 31?_____

_____

_____

6.   Reflect on this sequence: opened eyes (v. 31); burning hearts (v. 32); truth-sharing tongues (v. 34.)

C.   Jesus Carried into Heaven (24:36-53).

A careful study of this segment will be rewarded by many inspiring insights into the glories of the gospel. You may want to analyze the segment on an analytical chart. A few study questions are given below to start you along paths of inquiry. First read the segment carefully and prayerfully.
1.   Compare "in the midst of them" (v. 36) with "parted from them" (v. 51). Study the contexts of these phrases.
2.   Compare "peace" (v. 36) and "great joy" (v. 52).

How are the two related?_____

_____

3.   What miracle of verse 36 brought on the reaction of verse 37? _____

_____

What did Jesus do to convince the disciples that what they were beholding was real?_____

_____

4.   Read 24:44-49. Observe how Jesus connected the accomplished facts (death and resurrection) with the unfinished task (witness of these things).
5.   Observe Jesus' reference to the *Jewish* Scriptures (v. 44) and the *universal* gospel (v. 47).

6. How did Jesus involve His disciples in verses 48-49?

_____

What _specific_ command did He give to reveal that the disciples would soon embark on a new experience?_____

_____

7. Read 24:50-53. Visualize the action. Observe the bright references in each verse. How do you account for the transformation in the hearts of the disciples?_____

_____

8. Now that you have studied more of the details of the chapter, refer back to Chart DD and add some of your observations to the survey. Review the entire chapter and write a list of ten important spiritual lessons which this chapter teaches in such areas as faith, worship and witnessing.

III. NOTES.

1. Emmaus (24:13). The village was about seven miles from Jerusalem (direction not stated).* The exact location is unknown.
2. "Law . . . prophets . . . psalms" (24:44). Jesus is here recognizing the three parts of the Hebrew Bible (Law, Prophets, Writings). The name Psalms was used to represent the Writings, because Psalms was the prominent book of that group.

IV. ADVANCED STUDY.

Two important subjects for special study are suggested here: (1) the resurrection of Jesus; and (2) the Great Commission. Both are large subjects, and a study of either one would be a very rewarding experience. For the resurrection theme, consider such subjects as (1) proofs of the resurrection fact; (2) fruits of the resurrection faith. For the Great Commission theme, here are some subjects to

---

° Some old manuscripts read 160 furlongs, which would place Emmaus about 20 miles from Jerusalem. The shorter distance, however, fits the narrative better.

study: (1) the Commissioner; (2) the message; (3) the messenger; (4) the audience; (5) the outcome.

V. CONCLUDING REMARKS.

Man cherishes life, but his ship is wrecked on the rock of the grave. Luke as a medical doctor knew only too well how the miracle of life is marred by the tragedy of death. But Christ conquered death so that mourning could change to rejoicing. Even as Christians we need to be reminded of the victory that is ours in the *resurrected* Christ. We would profit by reading the angels' question as a rebuke to our own unbelief, "Why seek ye the living among the dead?" (24:5). If we are looking among the tombs for Jesus, we aren't the kind of witnesses He would have us to be.

* * *

Conclusion

We have come to the close of our study of Luke's gospel. We have learned to know more intimately the Son of man who came to seek and to save the lost. We have overheard Him pray; watched Him perform miracles; listened to His parables and sermons, and His more intimate instructions to His closest disciples. We have watched His enemies increase in number and in hatred, and have viewed His corpse on the despised tree of Calvary. And we have also seen Him as the resurrected One, restoring the circle of believers, and charging them with a mandate for worldwide witness.

Luke's next volume, the book of Acts, tells about the beginnings of that witness. We are living in the last days of that witness. Are we introducing the Son of man to the men around us?

Moody Press, a ministry of the Moody Bible Institute, is designed for education, evangelization and edification. If we may assist you in knowing more about Christ and the Christian life, please write us without obligation to: Moody Press, c/o MLM, Chicago, Illinois 60610.